FULL CIRCLE

fULL CIRCLE

by Natalie Allen

The Author's grandfather,
James Dymond Langsford outside his
packing shed at Brentswood.
The carter is George Morcombe.
c.1911.

Compiled from memories of
market gardeners of the Cotehele valley
and the diaries of Joseph Snell

Previous titles by the same author

S' Long Ago as I Can Mind
A Stitch in Time
Through The Letter-box

First published in 2000 by
Natalie Allen, Lampton House, Fairmead Road,
Burraton, Saltash, Cornwall PL12 4JQ

Copyright © Natalie Allen

ISBN 0 9508408 3 1

Typeset, printed and bound in Great Britain by
Latimer Trend & Company Ltd, Plymouth

Dedicated to
the Langsford family
and my grandchildren
Daniel, Matthew and Victoria

The Author's family tree from James Langsford (born 1771) to the present day

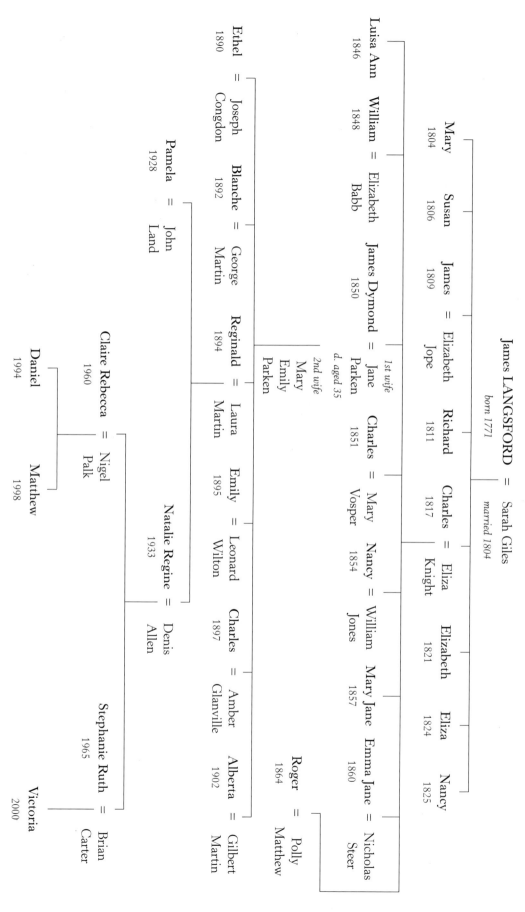

Contents

Acknowledgements

The author, Natalie Allen
(née Langsford). *c.*1999.

I wish to acknowledge the following magazines and newspapers consulted during the compiling of this publication: *Western Morning News*, *Western Evening Herald*, *Cornish Times* and *Grower*. I am grateful for the research facilities that were made available to me at the Evening Herald Picture Library, Plymouth, Liskeard Library, Royal Institution of Cornwall (Truro), also Dan DuPlessis, (Landulph), Alistair Tinto and Ann Murphy (St Dominick), Colin Squires (Saltash), Netta Jope (Callington), Iris Snell (Bere Alston), Alan Rowe (Yelverton), Richard Harnett (Kernow Nurseries).

I am indebted to all the villagers who contributed stories and photographs used in this book namely, George Brown, Derrick Cradick, Vera Duke, Tom Gorman, Aubrey Gale, Peggy Kusiak, Jean Laing, Peter Langsford, Inez Martin, Sylvia Mason, Jim Morrish, Alwyne Rickard, Francis Steer, Florrie Vinson, Gerald Veale and Courtney Vanstone.

Additional photographs were reproduced by kind permission of: Nexus Publications Ltd., *Western Morning News*, *Evening Herald*, Jennifer Graham, Pamela Land, Virginia Spiers, Mary Martin, James Evans, Josephine Kusiak, Nigel and Wendy Hunn, Aileen Fry, John Friendship, Alan Rickard, Kathleen Martin, Francis Congdon and Hazel Furse. A very special 'thank-you' to Phyllis Morrish for allowing me access to Joe Snell's diaries. Their very existence led directly to the publication of this book. Thanks to my 'cover-boys' George Brown, Courtney Vanstone and Derrick Cradick and to the photographer, Brian Carter.

Very special thanks to my daughter, Stephanie Carter for the typing of my manuscript on her computer and my son-in-law, Nigel Palk who organised, designed and created this book. He would like to acknowledge the support of his colleagues at the printers, Latimer Trend & Company Ltd, of whom Jon Flay and Mr W Bugler deserve special mention.

Preface

'A Jope lost 100 chicken and cows got in his front garden and George fell off his bike and the King died ...'

This entry in a diary dated 20th January 1936 immediately caught my attention. Written in pencil and barely decipherable in places, the small pocket diary was one of a collection which covered the period from 1914 to the day of the writer's untimely death in 1938.

These were the private diaries of one Joseph Snell, who spent his whole life working a market garden in the Parish of St Dominick in the Tamar Valley.

I felt very privileged to have been given the opportunity to go back in time and share the every day experiences of the man whose life, I was to discover, was so similar in many ways to that of my own parents. Both they and him, like others in the village made a living off the land, growing the fruits and flowers indigenous to the valley.

I had already spent many hours reading through some of the neatly written accounts and was intrigued by their content. Although lack of space only allowed a few words for any particular day, the life story of the whole village over a period of a quarter of a century was condensed into these meticulously kept records.

The most important thing that occurred in Joe's life on 20th January 1936 was the knowledge that his pal, A Jope of Berry Farm had suffered such bad luck on his farm, George had a mishap and the final noteworthy news on that day was the death of the King of England.

The order in which the news was related was typical of Joseph Snell. He always showed great concern for the health and well being of family and neighbours, yet managed to keep himself fully informed about national and world affairs. More importantly for those of us who still live in the area today; he kept an account of all the day to day incidents, which gained his attention.

Joe wrote the diaries and fortunately someone in his family treasured his memory enough after his death, to keep them safely for over 60 years until the time was right for their secrets to be revealed.

I was recently given permission by Joe's niece, Phyllis Morrish of Little Smeaton, to borrow these private diaries and to use exerts from them as part of my research into families in the Parish of St Dominick whose livelihood had been derived from the fertile slopes of the Tamar Valley.

Joe Snell's diaries not only gave details of his planting regime and the work carried out by his helpers, but provided a record of births, marriages, illnesses and deaths of parishioners and incidents as widely diverse as the sinking of the *Lusitania* off Ireland on the 7th May 1915 and the fact that Phyllis Jope wore her false teeth for the first time on the 12th September 1937!

I make no apologies for relating some of these varied items of news at intervals throughout this book ...

CHAPTER ONE

Down Memory Lane

by Natalie Allen

Few people who visit the village of St Dominick in South-East Cornwall, are aware that a building of archaeological interest is sited in their midst. I first came across this relic of a bygone era in 1985, whilst exploring a part of the village I had never visited before – Radland Mill Valley. A year or so before, whilst compiling 'A Stitch in Time', my book about the villagers of St Dominick, I had interviewed John Friendship at his cottage in Baber Lane. He had supplied me with a rich source of information and numerous photographs and items of interest. His memories are recorded in a chapter of 'A Stitch in Time', but now I had once again found myself in Baber Lane.

This time I parked my car and walked down Piper's Hill, a steep woodland track which eventually led to a stream over which at some period, a plank bridge had been erected, and on my right was Radland Mill. Over the years the sturdy mill building had been converted into a dwelling and it was still in very good repair, but now appeared to be used only as a weekend retreat. As the house was obviously unoccupied, I ventured through the overgrown garden.

So this was Radland Mill. It had been mentioned by a number of the people I had met during my earlier research, but at that time I had not had the opportunity to visit the area. The mill-wheel had long since gone and the mill-pool was choked with silt and weeds. There was no sign of the leat, which had carried the water from upstream to the wheel, when the mill was a going concern. The granite grinding stone had been incorporated into the front door step and this stone was now the only evidence that the building had indeed been a mill at some stage. The building looked sad and dejected and the fact that I had chosen a dull rainy day for my visit, added to the desolation.

Across the lane from the mill house, stood the remains of an old cottage and outhouses. Their roofs were gone and the stone walls were covered in green algae and moss, nurtured by the

My first glimpse of Radland Mill. c.1985.

constant drips of moisture which fell from the overgrown laurels which almost enveloped the ruins. Young saplings and ivy had taken root in crevices in the stonework and were well established. Already nature was doing her best to cover the tracks of man. I wondered whose hands had built these sturdy walls and how many years had elapsed since the cottage was last inhabited and who had occupied it over the years.

I followed the rough track around a sharp bend, past a spring that had obviously been the source of their water supply and there, on my left were the remains of another cottage, but this one had obviously been lived in more recently. Although its roof had caved in, the walls still stood to the height of the first floor and the rooms could be defined. No doubt this had been a cosy home for someone in the past.

Alongside the ruin was another stone built shed in reasonable repair, possibly intended as a stable or workshop. Beyond was a galvanised shed, which to my amazement still housed the remains of an old Ford truck. Over the years vandals had broken it's windows and lamps, and ripped out all the movable parts, but the chassis was still intact. Across the track was a tumbledown store with a cellar beneath and another stone building which, too, was roofless and open to the elements. Its main walls were partially demolished, but the strange thing about this shed was the way the inner gable-end was constructed. It was a single-storey building roughly 22 feet × 14 feet and of normal appearance from the outside, but the inside of the gable-end was built with four rows of staggered recesses set into it. Five recesses were built into the bottom row about 3½ feet from floor level, four in the next row, then as the gable-end narrowed, there were two more with a final alcove at the top, near the ridge. Each alcove measured roughly 15 inches high and 18 inches wide and was about 16 inches deep.

I had never seen anything like it before. What was its purpose, I was intrigued.

A feeling of mystery surrounded me. I stood there alone, a leaden sky barely visible through a thick canopy of leaves, the only sound the steady drip of raindrops and the gentle murmur of the stream.

There was nothing to prepare me for the story of Radland Valley, which was later to unfold …

Soon after my first visit to the hamlet of Radland Mill, I received a letter from a lady called Florrie Vinson, who lived in Devonport. She wrote to tell me she had very much enjoyed reading 'A Stitch in Time', and suggested that a sequel was in order! She even sent me some interesting photographs, so I arranged to visit her. To my surprise she informed me that she and her brothers and sister had spent their childhood in one of the cottages I had so recently discovered at Radland Mill! Further conversation led to me learning that a young lady named Amber Granville had also lived in the hamlet at one period with her grandparents, Mr and Mrs Arscott. Amber Granville was a name I knew well, for she was the wife of my father's only brother Charlie Langsford. I was astonished to find this link with my own family so early into my investigation.

I promised to keep in touch with Florrie, and to let her know if I ever decided to write 'A Stitch in Time' Part II!

———————————

A few weeks later, I was invited to give a talk to W.I. members at St Dominick Village Hall. In order to add a little interest to my talk about Bygone Days, I borrowed various items from those people who had contributed to my book. I had reason to visit Phyllis Morrish at Little Smeaton and in the course of our conversation, I mentioned that I had been exploring Radland Valley and Phyllis said her uncle, Joe Snell, had lived there for many years. Furthermore she unearthed a box full of diaries that had been kept by her uncle throughout his lifetime.

She was quite happy for me to borrow them and I spent many hours reading the tiny pocket diaries, in any spare moment I could find. After some time, I returned the diaries to Phyllis, but for some reason the very existence of these records, furthered my interest in Radland Mill.

After my conversation with Florrie Vinson, my thoughts often returned to the melancholy hamlet of Radland. That year I spent some time discovering the origins of the unusual building which had interested me so much, and my findings were published in an issue of 'Cornish Scene' in 1986.

Apparently, similar sheds were specially designed as a wintering house for bees and the unusual alcoves, called Bee-boles, were built to hold the straw skeps which were widely used in apiaries until the introduction of the portable wooden hives, in 1862. The early skeps were made of plaited straw, and did not last long in Cornwall's damp climate, so wintering houses were probably built as a dry home for over-wintering bees and as a store for empty bee skeps. There is every reason to believe that bee-boles were quite common in Cornwall in the 18th and 19th centuries and samples have been found in other parts of Britain dating from the 14th century. A bee-bole construction, similar to that at Radland, has recently been uncovered in the Lost Gardens of Heligan and can be viewed there. But over the years many have been destroyed and the owners of those still in existence, may well be unaware of their original purpose.

The building at Radland would have been constructed prior to 1800 and now, some two hundred years later it was semi-derelict and open to the elements and at the mercy of vandals. It was remarkable that the bee-boles at Radland Mill had survived the passage of time and were surely worthy of preserving. The Radland bee-boles have been recognised as being of archaeological interest and have been photographed and described in the International Bee Research Association Register of Bee-boles and were featured in an article in the 'Field' magazine in 1959. An earlier photograph clearly shows honey over flowing from a skep in the top-most alcove.

Solving the mystery of the unusual building, only served to increase my interest in the history of Radland Valley – what else would my investigations reveal?

THE SEEDS ARE SOWN

Many years were to pass before I once again returned to Radland. I became involved in the preservation of a 16th century cottage in Saltash, which was under threat, thus beginning a long association with the Tamar Protection Society, who are the custodians of Mary Newman's Cottage. This cottage is reputed to have been the home of Sir Francis Drake's first wife.

Bee-boles at Radland, prior to restoration. c.1985.

After spending many hours working on the fabric of the building with other volunteers I felt drawn to the plot of land behind the cottage which at that time was a wilderness of coltsfoot, brambles and bracken. Having previously rescued a cottage garden in similar circumstances at our own home, this was another challenge I was unable to resist and all my spare time over the next decade was spent creating and maintaining the garden at Mary Newman's Cottage. By the spring of 1989, the paths and steps were completed and the main part of the planting was flourishing and I had only the general maintenance of the garden to fill my hours.

Then the acquisition of an old photograph of a Cornish postmistress set my mind in motion and once more I set myself a new project. I decided to compile a book of postal history of

Cornwall as remembered by ex and present day postal workers. Fortunately, my husband had by this time taken early retirement and he was happy to drive me to various villages and towns all over Cornwall where I introduced myself to post office employees, young and old. After nine months of research I was able to publish my third book 'Through The Letterbox'.

Despite occasional gentle reminders from Florrie Vinson, the marriages of our two daughters and the subsequent arrival of two lively grandsons, along with my bed and breakfast business and voluntary work for Saltash in Bloom, left little time to consider compiling my half-promised sequel to 'A Stitch in Time'.

But one day I felt the need for a little solitude and I decided to return to Radland Valley. This time I approached from the bridlepath at Whitegate near Ashton. Once again I chose a wet, dismal day and as I squelched through ankle deep mud and water, I was overcome by a deep feeling of sadness as by now I knew a little more about the background of the land around me. By reading the old diaries, I had discovered that Phyllis Morrish's uncle, Joe Snell, had cultivated the surrounding land until his death in 1938, and that he and his sister Alice once lived in the ruined cottage opposite the bee-boles, which I had noted on my earlier visit.

As I approached the site of the bee-boles, I was amazed to discover that the whole building had been completely renovated and I was able to view the recesses through a window and it was obvious the bee-house had been expertly restored. The historic bee-boles were safe. However the little home I had noted earlier had been completely demolished and only the stone store remained intact. All evidence of the Snell's home had disappeared.

The mill house itself was obviously still occupied, but on that rainy day it was impossible to set aside the realities of scrubland and brambles and so visualise the hamlet as it must have been during the first half of the century. Then there had been no shortage of nectar for the bees, for the valley was filled with cherry, plum and apple blossom and beds of flowers were in bloom. Joe had devoted his whole life to his gardening and worked constantly in all weathers to provide the fresh produce, which made the Tamar Valley famous over the years.

I was reminded of the gardens at Brentswood that my parents had worked until the 1950s. Those too, have since been abandoned and the steep slopes planted with conifers. The tenants of Brentswood have all passed away and their way of life has become but a memory.

As I stood there, watching the rain drip relentlessly off the branches of a curiously misshapen fir tree, I remembered reading an entry in Joe Snell's diary,

'Planted 3 fir trees outside house'.

Even the fir trees had almost come to the end of their lives and I realised as autumn 1999 approached, that the time was ripe for me to harvest the last rich pickings. The village characters I hoped to talk to were, like me, reaching the autumn of their lives and their interesting stories deserved to be captured for future generations to enjoy. For life in the village of St Dominick will never return to the fruitful days so accurately recalled in Joe Snell's diaries and in the memories of his contemporaries.

My mind was made up. I contacted Phyllis Morrish and once more borrowed her uncle's diaries that had so inspired me 15 years before. I telephoned Florrie Vinson and said, "I've got the urge at last!"

"Well thank goodness for that, I haven't had an urge for years!" joked Florrie.

And so the seeds of 'A Stitch in Time' Part II were sown!

CHAPTER TWO

Joe's Garden

by Natalie Allen

Oh when a fellow loves a girl
And tries that girl to please,
He offers her his hand and heart
Upon his bended knee
Oh isn't he bewildered
When she turns her eyes aloft
And gentle whispers in his ear
Go home young man you're soft.

That verse was the first entry in Joseph Snell's 1914 diary and whether it related to an incident in his young life, for indeed Joe remained a bachelor all his life, or whether the verse amused him and he wished to retain it, no one now will ever be sure. His life and loves are but a memory and Joe rests peacefully in the churchyard overlooking the land to which he devoted his working days.

Joseph Snell was the second son of Benjamin Snell of Radland. His brother was also Benjamin and his two sisters were Alice and Mary. After Mary's marriage to Ernest Duke, Joe and his spinster sister continued to share a tiny cottage in the hamlet of Radland Mill where they tended about 18 acres of market garden.

Joe Snell

From records in his diaries it soon becomes obvious that they grew an amazing selection of produce on the south-facing slopes below Berry Road and also on land around their home and towards the Churchtown end of the valley. Practically every day was devoted to 'plowing', paring, weeding, planting and harvesting various crops. Besides the obvious daily routine of gardening, Joe took time off to collect coal and manure from the Works which at that time were still thriving at Halton Quay, or to fetch straw from Birchenhayes Farm or Haye Farm for bedding for his pigs and milking cow.

Punnets, chips and flower boxes had to be obtained from Fred Rogers's store at Pitt Meadow or in later years The Meadows near the village pub. Tools were taken to Mr. Hughes's blacksmith shop to be sharpened and his horse to Deacons at Paynter's Cross to be shod. There were visits to family and neighbours and also what was referred to as 'our annual trip' each June. On these occasions Arnold Jope always accompanied him and sometimes Fred Rabbage was invited to join them. It appears to have been an official, but more likely an unofficial contest to discover who in the parish had grown the best strawberries! The tour included visits to Comfort Wood, Brentswood and all the gardens in between. On 10th June 1926 the results were as follows: *H Maunder – The best, R Wadge – best 'baby-piece', W Cook – best 'earlies', S Striplin – best 'lates'.* So four growers were well pleased to have passed Joe's test and been rewarded for all their hard work, albeit by word only!

It seemed to be the normal practice for growers from one area to visit neighbouring gardens to compare crops but I think it was also a social thing as usually someone else was out and about for the same reason and a natter was the inevitable result. Joe often mentioned wandering down

Comfort Wood or to Sam Vosper's ground at Woodlands on the banks of the Tamar. These visits were reciprocated especially when Joe's passion for pollinating daffodils resulted in the production of a new variety. On 1st March 1938 Joe states *'1st Rich Cup seedling out'*. And a day or two later the entry reads; *'Mrs Williams, Tom Luxton, F Rabbage, Horace Renfree, H Hughes, Roy Rickard, Schoolmaster Watkin and party called to see daffodil'*. On 9th March the event warranted a visit from Martin Crufts who was a Dutch bulb salesman. A proud moment for Joe. He spent years cross-pollinating daffodils in the hope of producing a good marketable variety but unfortunately, Joe died before this particular new seedling produced enough bulbs to be viable. Another seedling he produced, flowered for the first time in April 1936 and he named it 'Market Glory'.

Every experiment he made, and there were hundreds, was carefully logged in the back of his diary in a form that appears obscure to the uninitiated.

Daffodils were not the only flowers grown at Radland. Listed were the names of a dozen or more varieties of Michealmas daisies, dahlias and spirea plus primroses, snowdrops, violets, tulips, iris, sweetpeas, gladioli, yellow daisies, wallflowers and snapdragons. Bundles of willow were harvested from an area behind the mill house and these were sent away by steamer in the early days and later by rail from Kelly Bray station, presumably for basket making. At Christmas time holly, ivy and laurel were offered for sale.

As for vegetables, the list was endless. Early and mid-season potatoes, turnips, leeks, savoys, sprouts, cauliflower, spring cabbage, tomatoes, cucumbers, broad beans, peas and runner beans. Even sage, mint and watercress were taken to market, perhaps making 1d a bunch. But every penny counted in those days and it all helped to pay the wages of his two full-time employees, Ward and Jack Matthews whose wage was shown to have recently risen to £1 a week! One entry, which appeared almost daily during August and September, concerned the marketing of runner beans. All the other vegetables were sold in pounds or stones but runner beans were always sold by the thousand. I had never come across this before. When I met Jim and Phyllis Morrish, I queried this and Jim said that 1,000 beans were approximately 20 lbs in weight and during the time that he and Phyllis had worked with Alice Snell at Radland after Joe's death that was the way the beans were sold. I don't know if this was the normal practice at this period or unique to Joe Snell.

During the season Joe and Alice and the 'boys' as he always referred to the Matthew brothers, would be regularly picking anything from 1,000 to 42,000 beans for market two or three times a week. Anyone who has grown runner beans will realise how labour intensive this job is and all the plants had to be staked using hazel sticks cut from the hedgerows.

His fruit included various eating and cooking apples, Early River, Czars and Victoria plums, damsons, grapes, figs, black currants, blackberries, strawberries, gooseberries, raspberries, rhubarb and both White Heart and black cherries. He also mentioned picking the first 'Duckey Hun' pears. I am unsure if this was a known variety or if it just referred to a particular tree, which he had perhaps, purchased originally from the Hunn family. Joe's diaries were full of little mysteries like this!

In July 1917 Joe notes that *'George Balsdon, Mrs Brailey, Charlie Ford, F & C Parkins, Harold Carkeet and J Lane picking cherries'*. So obviously he grew a lot of cherries at that period, providing, of course, that weather conditions were favourable. There was often mention of heavy and persistent rain that caused the cherries to crack and rot and starlings were also a menace, often clearing trees of fruit over night. On 12th July that same year Joe wrote *'Sold half ton raspberries'*. Another crop mentioned was 'Bishop's Thumbs' which Phyllis Morrish thinks were plums.

Joe also kept pigs that he usually bought at Callington market and he killed two or three a week for market during the winter months. They had a sty alongside their cottage but were also allowed to roam around a field during the daytime, where unfortunately they were not always content to stay. One incident upset our usually placid Joe and that day his diary read; *'Pigs had a day in Cotehele Woods and I went to football 'whinded' not in a good mood!'*

But Joe always supported the local football club and attended games and meetings and I think the highlight of his life was the occasion when St Dominick won the Bedford Cup! This event so impressed Joe that he devoted three days diary space to report the incident! This episode was written without one full stop as was usual; all Joe's daily happenings were linked with 'and' which made unintentional amusing reading at times, one such gem being, 26th January 1925. '*I brought home cross-cut from Striplins and Ern Duke cut my hair*'!

On another occasion he noted '*Brought back a handful of Horace bulbs from A Jopes and filled the hole in the sealen*' (ceiling).

So on the day of the Bedford Cup match on 6th May 1922 this is what he wrote: '*Went to Tavistock to see St Dominick win the Bedford Cup by beating Calstock 2–1. The Cup was filled by the Landlord of the White Heart Hotel with 'shampain' then the blue bell was decked with yellow and black ribbon then we proceeded to the hospital to show Edgar Langsford* the cup he congratulated the Team and shook hands all round then we left for Callington Finch the figurehead with the Cup on his knee to show … cheers were coming from every direction and arrived at Callington about 8 and the great crowd seemed delighted to think St Dominick had won … The cup was replenished at Golden's Hotel by L and J Trenance great numbers had a sip then tracks were made for St Dominick and a big crowd had gathered at Sheffield for the reception and the Cup replenished by A Jope and C Howard was the administrator and large numbers wet their whistle and by 10pm we all went home delighted*'.

Hardly a day passed without some reference to AJ (Arnold Jope) and his family of seven children who lived at Higher Berry, which was built by Arnold Jope in the early part of the century. Despite different life styles, Arnold being a family man and Joe a bachelor, their friendship endured throughout Joe's life and they obviously shared a variety of interests.

Joe Snell's diaries warrant a book in their own right such is their amazing content. The misdemeanours which befell some of the locals, births, baptisms, banns, weddings and deaths of what must have been the majority of the inhabitants of the parish were all noted. The names of the young men who enlisted for service in the First World War, those who appealed against conscription and sadly, all too often, the names of friends who gave their lives for their country. There were details of troop ships lost at sea, losses inflicted on the enemy and battles won and lost. Day after day in the autumn of 1918 was the sad news of victims of the flu epidemic that struck the village, including the deaths of Mr E Rogers's two young sons within a day of each other. There was news of the Great Strike and Joe's first sighting on 16th May 1918 of a sky ship drifting over Radland. On 25th January 1938 he described the unusual sight of the Northern Lights thus '*Saw Northern Lights about 6.30pm the sky was lit up red from east to west. At 10.30 as good as moonlight it looked like the dawn*'.

Surprisingly, when I looked at the entry on the day of the total eclipse 29th June 1927 the event caused no interest except for the one word '*Eclip*' at the beginning of his daily report and can think of no real explanation for this omission.

For those of you who might be interested, when Rev Streatfield preached for the first time at St Dominick Church on 18th August 1935 the 1st lesson was from Kings Chapter 18 and the 2nd lesson Matthew Chapter 11.

This small selection of information was interspersed with details of crop planting, harvesting and marketing. The sighting of the first swallow of spring, the arrival of the cuckoo and the date that Horace Jope and 'Look' (Luke) Hocking wore long trousers for the first time, which incidentally was on 13th May 1923!

Such was Joe Snell's interest in life.

---

*Edgar Langsford, one of their team-mates was recovering from a broken leg.

1914

Apr 20	My horse Tom ill.
Apr 25	Tom died of blood poisoning.
May 14	Liner *Empress of Ireland* bound from Quebec for Liverpool with 1307 souls on board was sunk in St Lawrence River the number of lives lost about 934.
June 10	FACT: each of the 8 Cornish Mayors who attended Royal Cornwall Show at Fowey is a total abstainer!
June 29	Started cherry picking full hands.
Aug 5	War declared against Germany.
Aug 14	Parkins, Congdons and Kelly's horses gone for War.
Aug 17	News of collision with the Bull Finch in which Henry Congdon killed.
Nov 3	Apples sent for North Sea troops.

1915

May 6	Uncle George and John went to Trematon.
May 8	News of the *Lusitania* sunk by submarine off Ireland.
May 13	St Dominick Fair.
May 27	News of *Triumph* sunk.
May 28	News of the *Majestic* sunk.
June 5	Went to Callington for Agricultural schemes.
June 21	Went to Callington and signed an agreement between Benjamin Snell and myself.
June 23	Mr Symons offering £10 per ton for gooseberries.
July 22	1000 beans 5/- Devonport market.
July 24	3000 beans 4/6 per 1000
July 25	Murder at Saltash.
Aug 8	E Duke and 2 Stephens joined 5 Bat DC Light Infantry. Duke's reg. number 2878.
Aug 10	E Duke came home in uniform.
Aug 12	Jack and Joe Snell (Ashton) went to see farm at Trematon.
Sept 7	Mrs Martin Towell died.
Sept 18	Beans dropped from 2/6 to 5d per 1000.
Nov 11	Gilbert and Ellice Islands in Pacific added to British Isles.
Nov 16	W Congdon, A Martin, H Wadge, N Grills, Mitchell, Ede, Ryder and P Bridgeman and S Mutton enlisted.
Dec 9	Planted 3 cypress trees in front of house.
Dec 10	Received notice to appear at recruiting office to be attested and to come under Lord Derby's recruiting scheme.
Dec 11	War fever A Jope, S Parkin, J Reep and F Rogers and hundreds of others enlisted.
Dec 17	Thatched the house.
Dec 30	J Matthews's birthday 15 years old.

1916

Mar 6	Went to Liskeard in snowstorm to appeal against Army service.
May 8	Locals appealing for exemption from War service.
May 9	Record bunches of flowers 1057 for market.
May 11	Picked 1st gooseberries 52 pounds.
May 12	Menagerie at Callington.
June 15	Sent off appeal papers.
July 1	Raised Jack's wages to £1.
July 5	Picked 1st cherries.
July 20	Children's Cherry Feast at Pentillie Castle. Overslept.
July 29	Germans drop bombs on East Coast of England.
July 31	Harold Carkeet came cherry picking.
Aug 2	Tosti Langsford joined Army.
Sept 20	Misses A and M Snell went Callington to 'right' books. (*Audit*).

CHAPTER THREE

When I received Florrie's letter telling me she had lived in St Dominick as a child and how much she had enjoyed reading 'A Stitch in Time', I had no idea she would be the person who would gently encourage me to write a sequel.

I have to admit I had never heard of the Taylor family until that letter arrived, not surprisingly really as the Taylor's left the village when I was very young.

The name was not one I had heard my parents mention, but by coincidence, when the Taylor's first came to live in St Dominick they lived in Radland Mill where my ancestors worked. Later they moved into a nearby cottage, which had previously been the home of a young girl Amber Granville, who was later to marry my uncle, Charlie Langsford.

Over the next few years Florrie wrote to me occasionally, hoping that another St Dominick book was on the press. At last the day arrived when I contacted her and told her I was seriously thinking of producing another book and she was delighted. Florrie has been a great help to me whilst I have been doing my research. Time after time I sent her lists of questions and back came the answers by return of post. Her enthusiasm and encouragement has been my inspiration and now I am happy to pass on some of Florrie's memories of her childhood, which she spent in the peaceful hamlet of Radland.

Childhood Memories

by Florrie Vinson (*née* Taylor)

My connection with St Dominick was severed many years ago, but even though I am 78 years old I still have very fond memories of my childhood, which was spent at Radland Mill.

I am Florrie Vinson born 31st August 1921. I now live in Plymouth. My maiden name was Taylor. My mother Florence was born in 1895 and she married William Taylor in 1915. My two older brothers, William and John were born in 1916 and 1917. My Father was in the Royal Navy and was away at sea a lot of the time. In 1923, when I was two years old, my parents, brothers, Grandfather Taylor and my Uncle Jack moved to St Dominick to live in the mill house in Radland Valley.

Our landlady was Bessie Langsford and the house was no longer in use as a mill at that time. I believe it closed many years before.

There were just two other cottages in the hamlet, one occupied by Mr and Mrs Arscott and in the other, up over the slope, lived Joseph Snell and his spinster sister Alice. My sister Dorothy was born at the mill in January 1925 and my youngest brother Charles arrived in May 1931. Soon after my sister's birth we moved across the lane to the cottage the Arscotts had vacated, Mr Arscott having died in 1922. Their grandchildren used to visit them at the cottage and their granddaughter Amber Granville lived there for a number of years as her parents had both died.

The Taylor family and friends from China, Mrs Carr and Billy outside their cottage. c.1928.

Mrs Taylor, William, Jack, Florrie and Dorothy at rear of Radland Cottage. Note the 'meat safe' on the wall. c.1928.

This cottage had five rooms plus a pantry and we had to fetch all our water from a trough fed by a spring just up the lane. We had a wonderful childhood at Radland; I shall never forget it. We used to fetch our milk from Mrs Striplin in Baber Lane and she was very fond of our baby brother and if we took him with us, she always gave him a little jug of cream all for himself. Richard Striplin was a carpenter and he also made the coffins and we always called him Dicky Box for that reason! He made a toolbox for my brother William and he still has it to this day.

It was sunny and bright down there when we were children, not overhung with trees and laurels like it is now. The area between the mill house and the lane was clear ground. We children used to play there and the boys held boxing bouts. There was a stone wall alongside the stream and the little wooden bridge was always known as First Bridge. The bridge fording the stream further down the lane towards the cottages at Berry was called Second Bridge.

So many incidents come to mind when I think back. We had a Bulldog called Chum and he used to go to Church School with us and everyone was scared of him. Sadly, in 1932 Uncle Jack accidentally ran over Chum and killed him.

Florrie, Dorothy and Charles Taylor with Chum and his friend. c.1932.

I remember that butcher Jim Reep's family had a little Peke called Swankey and it always barked at me when I went to Baber House for music lessons with Freda Reep. Mother paid 30/- (£1.50) a quarter for me to learn the piano and I got on very well. I was entered for a Trinity College music exam. It was held in the Old Athenaeum in Plymouth in 1934 and the adjudicator was Mr Weeks. He sat behind a book-laden desk in an enormous room and I was scared out of my life! However I'd won two certificates by the time I was fourteen and we moved into Plymouth to live.

My brother John (Jack) was very musical and he learned the violin and later clarinet, viola and saxophone and became bandmaster in the Royal Marines. After Jack married in 1943, he left the Royal Marines and went to teacher training college and later became Principal of Five-Mile Town School in Ireland. They lived there for 30 years and I visited them on one occasion. We were a very close family and never lost touch. I shall never forget Christmas 1967. Jack and his wife Rene came to spend Christmas with the rest of us and we had a real family reunion with turkey and all the trimmings. Jack printed a special 'joke' menu, which was very amusing, and all of us present signed our names on the back. I have always kept that momento which is especially poignant as our mum died in January 1968. Dad died in November 1969 so we were lucky to have had the opportunity to celebrate what turned out to be Mum's last Christmas.

When Jack retired he and his wife lived in Scarborough but came down here to celebrate their Golden Wedding in 1993. We visited all our old haunts, Whitegate, Halton Quay and Cotehele and had a lovely time together. Jack was very popular in Five-Mile Town. He used his musical ability to the full and formed a brass band and encouraged a lot of people to become musicians. Sadly Jack died in 1996, but many of his Irish friends travelled over to his funeral.

My other brothers and sister Dorothy are well and we often talk about our childhood memories.

Mother had a stall in Plymouth market where she sold a few eggs and whatever she could produce from our garden to bring in a bit of extra money. Mother always reared a pig and Frank Brown used to come down and slaughter it for us. We always kept poultry and Mum set up an

Easter Parade at Radland Mill. Florrie's mother and aunt Gladys Rowe. c.1927.

Jack and William Taylor and their sister Florrie, lived at Radland Mill in the 1920–30s Seen here re-visiting Halton Quay on the occasion of Jack's Golden Wedding in 1993. Jack died in 1996.

incubator in our front room and I used to help turn the eggs regularly and we watched the chicks being hatched. We fed our livestock with crushed oats, called euvago and this was stored in the barn beside our cottage. I loved it and would eat handfuls whenever I got the chance. I expect mice used to be in the shed running about, but I never came to any harm eating it!

Mother was never wealthy, she always made our clothes and she stayed up all night to finish knitting dresses for my sister and me for a special occasion. One was green and pink and the other blue and white I recall.

We used to go around the fields and pick primroses, which we sent to Covent Garden in London and received 9d, about 2½p for a dozen bunches. When I got older I remember that Joyce Martin worked at the Rectory and I used to scrub the back stairs for her and was paid 9d an hour. I was allowed to keep my wages and I bought myself a bike from Halfords for £1.19.11d (£2). Then I used to ride it to Bohetherick to bunch flowers. There was always a wonderful flower service held at the Church every year and all the children brought along their contribution. Alice Snell always sent up a selection of beautiful flowers from their market garden at Radland and the scent in the Church was unforgettable. Cecil Jane used to light the oil lamps that were hung on chains from the ceiling and he also wound the Church clock regularly. The Church was part of our life and I was confirmed in St Dominick Church by the Bishop of Truro, Maurice Keel back in Reverend Streatfield's time. I have a lustre ware jug which was purchased at Parson Square's sale at the Rectory in 1934. I recall seeing a cupboard full of vestments which had never been worn. Isn't it amazing what incidents stay in your mind over the years?

We always attended the annual Cherry Feast every July. It was held at Pentillie Castle at St Mellion. All the children in the neighbourhood were invited and many travelled miles by horse and wagon or on foot to reach there. We had a feast of cherry pie and cream served at long tables on the lawns of the castle. Afterwards, races were arranged and we played games like hide and seek and hopscotch and we would pull each other down steep slopes on a sack.

Sometimes we went to Plymouth on the ferry to visit our granny and often, after Sunday school we would walk to Cotehele Quay past Mr Trenance's plum orchards. Another pastime was collecting chestnuts from outside the Churchyard. That tree is now incorporated in the newest part of the Churchyard.

We children attended the Church School and Miss Moon was our teacher and we were given a very good education. When Miss Moon died, aged 58 in 1932 all the school children attended her funeral and we sang 'Days and moments quickly flying'. My brother Bill always gave credit to his school and he went on to learn a trade as an electrician with J W Davis in Plymouth. He then went into the Navy and became Chief Electrician and specialised in torpedo work.

Rear of Taylor's cottage, seen from Piper's Hill. c.1928. Today it is a complete ruin.

William and Jack Taylor,
Joe Snell's protégées.
c.1926.

A strange coincidence comes to mind about that. We, as a family, often found ourselves returning to Radland Mill to look around the place where we were so happy. On one occasion we were standing on the bridge just looking at our old home and a gentleman came out of the mill house and spoke to us. Do you know, he was the Chief Telegrapher on the same ship as my brother Bill had served on and they knew each other! We were invited into the mill house for tea and a chat.

I have only one unhappy memory of my childhood at St Dominick. This occurred when a child called Lorna died. We went into a darkened room and saw her lying in her coffin and the memory has never left me. But mostly our life was joyful.

Joe Snell was a lovely man and very well liked. He lived in the same cottage all his life, but the mill house saw a lot of comings and goings. From 1918 until our arrival in 1923 a Mr Braund lived there and after we moved across the lane in 1925 the Davy family went there. Then Will Bennett was there for a while with his five children – he was an Estate Agent in Plymouth and moved around a lot. I also remember the Hambridges and Mr and Mrs Williams. The house is still occupied now I believe, but our cottage and outhouses were condemned years ago and are now in ruins. The Snell's house is also demolished, but the outbuildings still remain intact.

Joe Snell was a self-taught boxer and he introduced Jack and William to boxing. They used to box at the Blue Cap Hotel at Callington and got paid 5/- to fight three rounds. The boys used to enjoy fishing in the stream and Jack was especially good at 'tickling' a trout. He would throw them up on to the bank and it was my job to thread string through their gills. One day the boys found a stranger fishing in the stream near Whitegate. They got talking and he told them he was the Great Houdini

Phone:
St. Dominic 33   Church Town, St. Dominic, Cornwall,

193

M

Dr. to **TAYLOR'S GARAGE.**

GENERAL CARRIERS TO AND FROM PLYMOUTH,
TUESDAYS, THURSDAYS, & SATURDAYS.

Bus Services between Callington, Harrowbarrow & Gunnislake Station.

Taylor's billhead.

Taylor's lorry. c.1926.

and was appearing at the Palace Theatre in Plymouth. When I told Natalie this, she was unable to confirm it so perhaps it was someone having the boys on! It's a good tale anyway!

I used to go to school with Joe Snell's niece, Phyllis Duke and I still have a school photo with us both in it. Another thing I always remember are the bats – there were always lots of them flying around at dusk and a white owl made its home in the old stone barn across the stream, but I seem to remember that it got killed and ended up in a glass case in the Jope's house.

Uncle Jack ran a business as a carrier and he had a covered lorry, which he kept, in a shed just inside Whitegate. He used to cart goods to and from Plymouth. Some of us children used to ride in the cab when Uncle Jack drove around the village collecting marketing from outside our customers homes to sell at Plymouth Market. I used to help work out the commission and prepare the accounts, which Uncle Jack then paid to the growers. In 1925 he bought a bus called 'One and All', this was printed on the rear in large letters. He employed a driver and the bus travelled between St Dominick, Harrowbarrow and Gunnislake Station. He advertised the carrier service in the 1933 Doidges Annual I recall. Uncle Jack worked very hard and he died in 1939 when he was only 39 years old.

A young 'conductor', Charles Taylor aged three in J F Taylor's Chevrolet bus, known as 'One and All'. c.1934.

My grandfather died whilst we were at Radland and we moved up to Churchtown where we lived in the house just up from the Post Office where Postman Howard once lived. This property had a large garage and Uncle Jack and Mr Striplin built a shed to house two vehicles. My brother fixed us up with electricity, which was run by a generator, and we were very proud of our new electric lights. Polly's sweet shop was next door and Uncle Jack used to give me three pence for 3d worth of 'aporths'. When Polly died one of the Jope girls married Luke Hocking and lived there for some time.

In 1935, Dad left the Navy and had a job at the Royal Naval Hospital at Devonport, so we had to make our home back in Plymouth. Mother nearly had a mutiny on her hands when we heard we had to leave St Dominick, we all loved our life in the Village. We have never forgotten our happy childhood at Radland Mill and I have really enjoyed thinking back and remembering all the little things that gave us such pleasure when we were young. It would be lovely to meet up with some of the friends we knew in the old days and have a really good chat together. I have often wondered how we came to move to St Dominick all those years ago, how on earth did Mother discover Radland Mill? I never thought to ask Mum about it when she was alive but I am very glad she did choose to live in the little house in the woods, they were such happy days.

1917

Jan 12	J D Langsford called for Income Tax.
Jan 16	4 inches of snow pruned out cherry trees Watergate field.
Jan 18	Mr Lloyd George and Admiral Beatty celebrated their birthdays. LG. 54 Beatty 46 and keeper Cox died.
Jan 24	H Langsford bought Glamorgan Mill.
Jan 26	Village of Hallsands (Devon) swept away in great storm.
Jan 27	Last day for Worth commanding steamer.
Feb 3	Cabin on fire and steamer stuck at Cotehele.
Feb 5	Ward Matthews received calling up papers.
Feb 24	Potato riot at Devonport.
Mar 8	Started planting strawberries in Pond field planted 160 gooseberry cuttings
Apr 10-12	White with snow windows sheet of ice.
Apr 23	Heard cuckoo 1st time.
Apr 24	Saw 1st swallow.
May 5	Put in 8 row Bedfordshire prize cucumbers 3 row king of Ridge and 3 row Stockwood Ridge in frame.
May 17	St Dominick Fair.
May 18	Over 1000 bunches of flowers for Devonport Market.
May 20	A J and I had our annual fruit garden inspection.
May 21	Started picking gooseberries and sticking beans.
May 24	L Trenance and Hoskin each spoke of a ripe strawberry.

June 10	A J ordered 2 pair of trousers.
July 15	Baptism of Marg, Joe Congdon's daughter.
July 18	Hard rain cracked cherries.
July 31	Saw wrecked train other side Saltash.
Aug 29	Duckey Hunn's pears ripe to perfection.
Sep 7	Picked first lot of grapes.
Sep 13	Sad news of C Ford killed in action.
Sep 14	22 dozen Damsons for market.
Sep 16	Charles Langsford died. (Harold's father).
Sep 19	Started picking apples.
Sep 25	Earl of Mount Edgcumbe died.
Oct 3	Bought 12 pigs 36/- each.
Oct 14	Saw AJ's baby boy for first time.
Nov 5	News of Captain Vanstone killed in action.
Nov 9	News of Tosti Langsford killed in action.
Nov 22	J Snell and Miss Bessie Chubb married.
Dec 25	E Duke came home from France.

Tosti Langsford of Cleave Farm. c.1911.

General Information

24th February 1917

The only entry in Joe's diary on that date filled me with alarm! 'Potato riot at Devonport.' I decided that this incident warranted further investigation, so I set off to Plymouth Library where I was able to examine newspapers of that period. Sure enough, there was the report, but I soon realised that nothing too violent had occurred at the market that day.

The cause was a potato shortage, which meant that only three or four growers had potatoes for sale and buyers, 'rushed in a light-hearted manner' to obtain a share. The market authorities thought it would be a wise precaution to involve the Police, so one Inspector and several Constables, were placed on duty at the market and they ensured that everyone formed an orderly queue. Each buyer was limited to half a stone each at 1/9d a stone. Some disappointed customers left the market with nothing, and on meeting a man coming along the street with a sack on his back, assumed he was a potato grower and they quickly followed him back to a market stall. When he emptied his sack, it was found to contain turnips! Similar incidents occurred at Plymouth market too, when five market gardeners, offered just 10 bags of potatoes for sale, a quarter of the normal supply. It seems that retailers were not allowed to charge more than one and a half pence per pound by law, so they put a condition on their customers, insisting that if they wanted to buy potatoes they also had to purchase a small turnip or an orange at an inflated price – they were charging 3d. for one walnut!

Two days later, Joe mentions planting 30 rows of Sharps Victor potatoes, thus ensuring a plentiful supply for market next season!

Courtesy of Western Morning News.

24th September 1917

'Nine soldiers cut to pieces at Bere Ferrers.'

This account in Joe's diary resulted in me discovering a harrowing report in an old newspaper. It appears that a train carrying troops on the London and Southwest railway came to a halt on the up-line just outside Bere Ferrers's station. Some of the soldiers, under the impression that at the first stop they were to be served with rations, left the train. As they jumped down onto the line, they were immediately struck by an Express train travelling at 40mph.in the opposite direction and killed instantly. Nine died on the spot and three others were seriously injured. Had the Express train been a few seconds later, many more might well have been alighting from the troop train. The survivors were instructed to retrieve the remains of their dead comrades, and with the help of railway officials, they conveyed them to the goods depot at the station.

Here again is proof, if indeed proof is needed, of the accuracy of Joe's accounts of everyday occurrences. Practically every incident that has been mentioned to me during my research for this book can be verified by a glance at Joe's diary on the relevant date.

Courtesy of Western Morning News.

Daffodils planted

The following varieties of daffodils were amongst those grown by Joe Snell in the mid-1930s.
Poet, Snow Icing, Dachye, Killigrew, Martin's Fancy, Kitchener, Beresheba, Cheero, Forerunner, Princess Astride, Havelock, Village Beauty, Silver Salver, The Prince, Nimrod, Smero, Irma, St Bernard.

Names of Michealmas daisies planted by Joe Snell at Radland on 7th March 1925.
Snowdrift, Acme, Pink Pyramid, Maid of Athens, Rudolph Goethe, Alderham Pink, King George, Harmony Lavender, Maggie Perry, Louvain, Blue Star and *Golden Glow.*

CHAPTER FOUR

The Mills of Cotehele

by Natalie Allen

The first mention of a corn mill at St Dominick was in the Will of one Tristram Tibb in 1629. That mill was situated in Radland Valley, but it was not until 1820 that the Langsford name featured in the records, as a miller at Radland Mill. It was this information that led me to discover my ancestral background.

James Langsford born in 1771 had married Sarah Giles in 1804 and by 1825, they had eight children. James was very poor and he did not own the mill, it was leased from Edmond and Joseph Snell. The Snell family owned most of the land around the Radland Valley at that period.

One of James and Sarah's children, Charles, born in 1817, married Eliza Knight in 1845 and they, too, had eight children, Louisa Ann, William, James Dymond, Charles, Nancy, Emma Jane, Mary and Roger. Louisa died when she was seventeen and Mary when she was an infant.

On the death of his father in 1844, Charles inherited the business and the remaining years of the leasehold on the mill. James's other children received five shillings each in his Will. Charles continued to work Radland Mill, as did his young sons William and James Dymond. However, the 1871 census states that Charles was now a miller at Morden Mill*, which had previously been worked by the Dymond family and an eighteen year old son, also named Charles, was described as a miller too. Charles's eldest son William stayed on at Radland Mill and lived there with his wife Elizabeth and his two sons, Ernest and Charles and four young daughters. James Dymond later married Jane Parken and they lived at Birchenhayes Farm. James Dymond was my paternal grandfather.

Soon after this the leasehold of Radland Mill expired, having been with the Langsford family for over fifty years. Around 1880 Radland Mill ceased to be a going concern and the mill building became a private dwelling house. I came across a difference of opinion, when I tried to discover where the Langsford family lived in those early days, some think they lived in the cottage which once stood opposite the mill building, where the Taylor family lived during the 1920s and 30s and this may well be true. However, Peggy Kusiak told me that her mother, Dorothy Maunder, *née* Langsford, had taken her to the area as a child, and shown her the ruins of the Langsford home. Old maps do show another property in the area, known as Radland Clift, so maybe that was the original home of James Langsford's family. The mill building is the only habitable dwelling in the hamlet today, the other two cottages having been condemned some time ago.

Charles Langsford senior (1817–1902) and Emma Jane Langsford. c.1870s.

*Morden Mill is also referred to locally as Murden Mill or Cotehele Mill.

From top left: 'Black Cook',
Charles Langsford,
Nelson Langsford,
John L Avent, and W Ball.
Bert Langsford, Mary Vosper
with baby Dorothy,
Mabel Langsford,
Stanley Langsford,
Horatio Langsford.
(Note the bugle).
Lady (not known),
George Langsford,
Albert Langsford,
Harold Langsford. *c.*1894.

When Charles Langsford senior, took over Cotehele Mill, it was just a corn mill, two-storeys high, with two millstones, but between 1876 and 1890 big improvements were made. New stores and workshops and a bake-house were built and a second water wheel set up to drive a saw-bench. Five bar gates etc., were made there, also punnets and boxes for the fruit trade. Charles junior was very much involved in the mill at this stage. Although the property was rented from the Earl of Mount Edgcumbe, the extensions were built at the expense of the Langsford family.

The punnet factory closed in 1924, but the sawmills carried on until about 1930. A baker, John Avent, from Plymouth was employed to work in the bakery and he boarded with the Langsford family in the miller's house. Bread, tufts and saffron cakes were produced daily and delivered around the parish in a covered trap. As each son became old enough, they drove the trap and they blew a bugle to announce their arrival. In the 1891 census Nelson Langsford, aged fourteen was listed as 'a bakery delivery boy'. (Nelson Langsford was great-grandfather to Ruth Langsford the

Langsford's Bakery Cart.

Harold Langsford's first
Morris commercial truck
outside Murden Mill.
The galvanised shed (now
demolished) was part of the
sawmill. c.1930.

television personality). The bakery always provided bread and cakes for the Anniversary tea at the Wesleyan chapel and also supplied Cotehele House. The butler and housekeeper were Mr and Mrs Coulter. Mrs Coulter was a stern lady of impressive appearance in her rustling black silk dress and chatelaine but they always gave the baker boy some refreshments in the servant's hall.

Charles junior, married Mary Vosper in 1874 and they had thirteen children, two of whom died in childhood.

In 1880 Charles senior, ordered the nearby Glamorgan Mill to be rebuilt. The original granite doorframe was left intact and the date 1717 and initials T.D. seems to indicate another connection with the Dymond family. One Thomas Dymond was miller at Morden (Cotehele) Mill in 1678. The Dymond's were well established in St Dominick during the period 1379 to 1871. Records show the family resided at Smeaton and Stockwell during that period, but the name died out in the village in 1871. There may well be a family connection between the Langsford's and the Dymond's, hence my grandfather's second christian name.

A Mr Boney, who was also involved with the building of the Calstock viaduct, supervised the building work at Glamorgan. It cost three hundred pounds to re-build the mill including the cost of a new waterwheel supplied by Jabez Buckingham of North Hill.

When Charles senior died in 1902, his Estate was valued at over £8,000, a vast amount more than his father James was able to accumulate in the whole of *his* lifetime. It is not known how Charles accrued so many assets over those few years in the milling business and it is thought he may have inherited money from another source. In his Will, Charles senior, left Radland Mill, which he had previously purchased from the Snell family, to his grandson Ernest, as his eldest son William had pre-deceased him. In his lifetime Charles had also purchased Glamorgan Mill and some land, from the Mount Edgcumbe's. He also owned six cottages at Metherell and Cleave Farm. These properties and other cash assets were shared amongst his five surviving children. Charles's wife, Eliza, died in 1903.

Members of the Langsford family kept both mills in production over the next few years. Charles junior died at Stockwell in 1917 aged 65 and in that year one of his sons, Harold purchased Glamorgan Mill from his cousin's widow Amy Langsford, for £1,000. Harold and his wife Dorothy *née* Cradick, whom he had married in 1914, were at that time living in the miller's house, alongside Cotehele Mill. They had four children, Marie, Nancy, Peter and Joyce. In 1938, Harold and his family moved to the house at Bartletts which he had previously purchased and both mills continued to work during the war years.

When I first visited Peter Langsford regarding the history of the mills, I was shown the family tree and numerous photographs. But as our talks continued, various other details emerged. Over tea and biscuits I was entertained with tales of his childhood and amusing family incidents. Names, which I had heard mentioned over the years, began to gain substance, as I slowly began to link together the infamous members of the Langsford clan! So many of the villagers I interviewed mentioned the fact that their great-grandfather was Charles Langsford and I have now come to the conclusion that our great-grandfather, Charles senior sowed the seeds of all the present day inhabitants of St Dominick! But perhaps I exaggerate just a bit!

One amusing incident, that Peter assures me is true, concerned the bakery. This building had been purpose built near the waterwheel at Cotehele Mill but now there is little evidence of its existence. The building had contained a large brick oven, which was heated by inserting faggot wood into the aperture and setting it alight, the iron door was then closed and when the wood had burnt out the door was opened and the ash was removed. The bread and cakes were placed in the hot kiln and left for the appointed time. After Mr Avent left, a new baker was employed and one-day Peter's mother saw him shaving. To her dismay, she realised he was soaping his beard with the same brush as was in daily use in the bakery to glaze the products prior to baking! He appeared quite unconcerned, but Peter's mother was not impressed and the bakery did not survive for long after that little incident. It closed down in the latter part of the First World War.

In 1926, an electricity supply, bathroom and flush toilet were installed at the Langsford's home at Cotehele Mill. Prior to this water was heated in the wash boiler and dipped out into an old cast iron bath. This only happened on Fridays but that was a great improvement on the washing habits of Peter's great-grandmother who, it was said bathed 'once a year *if* it was necessary!' Power was generated by the waterwheel but was only powerful enough to produce a 50-volt supply. This was sufficient for lighting the house and Peter's mother was said to have been shocked to see just how dusty her home was, when it was first illuminated by electricity, as opposed to the less powerful oil-lamps! She bought an iron, a kettle and a specially adapted cleaner, but none of these pieces of equipment could be used simultaneously, or the house would be plunged into darkness! However, his mother was very well pleased with the modern improvements.

When Charles Langsford was expanding his business in the late nineteenth century, the road from Cotehele Bridge to the two mills was still not much more than a woodland track and the approach road from St Dominick to Cotehele Mill was via Oak Tree. Part way down the steep Morden hill, the road branched to the right and the track for horses and carts then emerged just about opposite the mill building. Peter recalls that Henry Collins used to regularly bring his steam engine down to the bottom road (New Road) and roll in sand and stone. But because water was always draining from springs in the woods, this soon washed away again and cartwheels left deep ridges on the track. Charles Langsford junior and other nearby tenants paid a sum of money towards improving the road, which was later adopted by the Council.

Good maintenance was also essential to keep the mill working on a daily basis. In the early days, when cogs or buckets needed replacing this meant Jim Goard from a St Germans firm of engineers and millwrights, spending a few days working on the wheel and machinery. The Langsford's provided accommodation on these occasions and according to Peter, he was a very polite gentleman and very appreciative. On being offered an extra portion of food he would reply, "I have had elegant sufficiency, Mam."

Peter was the last to manage Cotehele Mill and it ceased to operate in 1960. At that time, it's owners, The National Trust, resumed responsibility for it and it is now a visitor attraction and open to the public in conjunction with nearby Cotehele House and Garden.

Glamorgan Mill is now a private house and although the exterior has not been altered to any great degree, there is little evidence of its past use. Only a few locals still remember, Monty Rogers, Pikey Rich, and Charlie Sambles and all the other men who were employed by the Langsford family over the years.

I am indebted to Peter for supplying family memories and a copy of the family tree. The Langsford's were well represented in the village in the 20th century and I could not have compiled this chapter without the information obtained from him. Peter's father died in 1974 and Peter remained a bachelor, so there are no sons to carry on the family name in Harold's branch of the family tree.

In a following chapter Peter records his experiences during and after the Second World War and so brings to an end the Langsford's story and their 150 years as millers in the Tamar Valley.

1918

Jan 3	Planted pear gribbles in the wood.
Feb 24	Went to Stoke Climsland to see Prince of Wales.
Mar 18	Started to build greenhouse bricks sand lime from Kelly Bray.
Mar 23	Heard news of great attack on Western Front.
Apr 4	Mr F Braund and family come to Radland Mill to live.
Apr 7	F Rogers bought a motor car.
Apr 30	Sid Mutton, Tink, Cook, Worth, Paynter, Nattle, and Martin Heathfield passed out A1, E Rickard not A1
May 19	Great air raid in London.
June 3	Gooseberry prices controlled and fixed at 27/- cwt.
June 9	Bought swim costume.
June 25	Heard Gormans took Tipwell Farm.
July 4	George Hawke fined 5/- for being drunk and G Hocking £2 for leaving carcass unburied.

July 28	Cherries 1/6 per pound wholesale at Devonport Market.
Aug 20	Price of small apples fixed at £12 per ton.
Aug 26	Swimmed length of bath with wings.
Aug 29	Filled 4 bee butts.
Oct 16	J Congdon's farm (Mutton Mill) sold £4250 to Mr Northmore.
Oct 18	Went to Balfour Hall Plymouth to be medically examined and had photo taken.
Oct 21	Mrs Fry (Rosie Roberts) died flu. Filled out form (Food Production for 1919) and undertook to cultivate 12 acres. Potatoes 4 acres, fruit and garden 6½ root and green crops 1½ to keep 1 cow and sell no milk.
Nov 6	Went Rogers's double funeral of his sons.
Nov 11	War ended Church bells ringing everywhere.
Dec 13	Brought home 2000 raspberry cane from Leonard Cradick.

Wedding of James D Langsford's eldest daughter, Ethel. 8th June 1915.

Back row: Reginald Langsford, Miss Martin (Burcombe), Parson Square, Charlie Langsford, Emily Langsford, James Dymond Langsford. *Front row:* Mrs Bridgeman, Lily Congdon (bridesmaid), Joseph Congdon and his bride Ethel, Alberta Langsford (bridesmaid) and Mary Emily Langsford (bride's mother). The dress worn by the Bride's mother is now in the possession of Kathleen and Stuart Martin of Towella, St Dominick.

Middle row: Mary Congdon, R Congdon, Blanche Langsford.

CHAPTER FIVE

A Feast of Information

by Natalie Allen

In this modern age it is the usual practice to spend some time each summer, touring around some previously unknown region.

This year, 1999, I decided to do the same, but I suffered no traffic jams or hold-ups at airports; neither did I experience jet lag on my return; but never the less I visited new places; increased my knowledge of the area and enjoyed the services of both a private chauffeur and a personal guide.

I went to Bohetherick! My chauffeur was my long-suffering husband and my guide a man who has spent all his life living and working in the village of St Dominick … Courtney Vanstone.

I have known Courtney for over fifty years dating from the period when we all spent our wild youth dancing away the night at the Blue Cap Ballroom in Callington – but that's another story. Now Courtney's wild days are over, as indeed are mine and we were quite content to spend our time talking about the old days. We walked through woods which until a few decades ago, were the working place of hundreds of villagers who earned their living market gardening in the Cotehele Valley.

As a child living on a farm called Birchenhayes, I had often visited both Glamorgan and Murden Mills at Cotehele with my dad, Reginald Langsford. We went there to collect crushed oats and bran for our livestock. I had heard of 'Comfort 'ood' and 'Cudeal' 'ood' and was aware of various market gardens beyond those of our own at Brentswood. So on this warm September day as Courtney and I wandered around, the names of people and places my parents used to mention began to come to life for me.

Courtney Vanstone transporting 2 lb chips of strawberries in a large four-sided carrier. These home-made wooden carriers were in common use in market gardens and were constructed in such a way as to allow a man to stand in the centre and lift the structure by two woden handles. As the weight was evenly distributed, large quantities of fruit or flowers could be carried in this way. A short supporting leg at each outer corner, enabled the carrier to be placed on the ground whilst being loaded, without fear of damaging crops. c.1955.

As a 'local', Courtney was known by everyone and he was able to take me to places I would not otherwise have been able to visit without permission, many of which were foreign to me as I had never had reason to visit them before. One such venue was to Woodlands, a picturesque house with wonderful views of the River Tamar. The residents happened to be away on the day in question but Courtney assured me that Andrew Veale would not mind if we took a quick look at the nearby land. He took me to see the rusty remains of a shed which had once housed a large boiler and this had been used to make jam, using the surplus plums and strawberries which had flourished in the gardens during the period when Mr Sam Vosper resided at Woodlands. This little factory came about during a period in the 1930s when production out-stripped demand for fresh fruit, so to utilise the spare fruit and provide another source of income, this family diversified into the preserving business. Courtney also pointed out another little cottage across the valley below Haye Farm, which he said was always known as the Jam House, so no doubt jam was produced there too.

The commencement of the Second World War meant that food imports were restricted and growers were then expected to use their land to it's full capacity to produce food crops so the fruit market became more profitable again. The Tamar Valley produced an enormous quantity of fruit and vegetables to help feed the nation, there was no more surplus fruit so the jam factory was no longer needed and fell into dis-use. The daffodil market flourished too due to the lack of imported flowers. However growers faced a fine if they did not comply with the order to grow more edible crops and 'Dig for Victory'. Consequently, many acres of daffodil bulbs were dug up and replanted on banks and hedgerows leaving the land free for the cultivation of food products. These bulbs still flowered despite the lack of attention and to this day many of the old varieties are still blooming.

As we stood outside the old jam shed looking across the fields towards Haye and beyond, Courtney recalled the time when all these fields had been orchards. Apples, plums, pears and cherries had flourished there and according to a map I obtained dated 1904 there were vast areas of orchards all over St Dominick

Margaret Vanstone and Mrs Cundy. c.1955.

and neighbouring villages. Every farm had its own orchard and many farmers made their own cider or else sold their crops to cider producers. Now most of the orchards have died out as supermarkets insist on fruit of uniform shape and size irrespective of flavour and there is little demand for the varied fruits which have been grown locally for generations. Fortunately, we have someone living in the village who still values these old types of apples and cherries. James Evans and his partner, artist Mary Martin, have in recent years rescued many of the old varieties by grafting young trees and planting up a new orchard on land which they own in the valley. It is good that someone still cares enough to grow these trees for future generations to enjoy.*

Most of the old orchards are now merely grass fields, with just the occasional lichen covered apple tree standing forlornly, a sad reminder of more fruitful times.

After leaving Woodlands, we started to make our way to Cotehele Bridge passing on the way the neatly kept acres now worked by Gerald and Joyce Veale, whose memories can be found in chapter twelve of this book. We passed the entrance on the left of the road, which led to land known as East Down. A well-known St Dominick family, the Trenanaces once worked these gardens and hundreds of plum trees were grown there. After the Trenances retired their two sons-in-law, Francis Hunn and Harold Harris took over the land. A few yards further down the road on the right-hand side are fertile slopes that run down to the marshes (or 'mash' as we 'locals' call them) on the River Tamar. This is Cherry Gardens, worked by Joe and Jim Trenance at one-time. Cherry and plum trees, which once filled the valley with blossom, have been replaced by row upon row of eucalyptus trees, a crop which can be seen in most of the few remaining gardens in the parish. This is a crop which Courtney feels is being over produced, not only in this village, but all over Cornwall. He fears that growers will kill the trade by over production as this shrubby foliage has now overtaken the once popular pittosporum trade.

---

*See "Burcombes, Queenies and Colloggetts" by Virginia Spiers.

Stan and Alec Sleep were among those who worked in Cherry Gardens after the Trenances. One section was always known as 'Vanstone's Field' but Courtney doubts if it was named in honour of *his* family!

The land is now tended by Norman Searle and like most of the remaining market gardens is fully mechanised. Gone are the days of hand digging and hoeing.

By this time we all felt in need of nourishment and our guide directed us to the Carpenters Arms at Metherell with such skill that I got the impression he might have already been familiar with this particular hostelry!

After we were suitably refreshed we once again returned to the grand tour. We retraced our steps to Bartletts and took the steep hill ahead, which finally led past Berry Farm and down to Whitegate. This time I was on more familiar ground as I had recently followed the bridle path from Whitegate into Radland Mill on a number of occasions whilst discovering Joe Snell country. However, Courtney had not been down to this hamlet for many years and was amazed to see how the land had reverted to woodland since last being cultivated in 1965. We chatted as we made our way along and Courtney told me that the Snell family had grafted apple trees in the past and at least one of these was named after the Snells – Snells White. We took a look at the remains of the two ruined cottages where Joe and the Taylor family once lived and saw the mill house which through the years had remained occupied for the majority of the time, having changed hands many times since it was last used as a corn mill by the Langsford family. After returning to Whitegate we drove the short distance to Spur House, mentioned so many times in Joe's diaries. It was here that Frank and Beatie Rogers had lived and they had worked about two acres opposite the entrance to nearby Eastcott. After Frank Rogers's time Albert Allen took over followed in later years by John Bailek. This land is no longer cultivated and is a meadow.

Following our little diversion into Radland Mill we returned once more to the Cotehele road over Boars Bridge. The origin of this name remains a mystery to me and I had not heard of it until I met up with George and Freda Brown and heard how they had worked five and a half acres across the stream at Boars Bridge. We passed Newhouses, where in the past Jack and Mary Langsford and their daughters Pauline and Molly had lived. We parked outside the entrance to Comfort Wood. I had heard this place mentioned so many times in my childhood, but strange as it may seem I had never discovered its exact whereabouts until today.

"Tis a good job I'm yer to take 'ee around about" joked Courtney, and I had to agree!

We entered the welcome shade of the wood and once more Courtney gave me a lesson in local history.

"My father told me that until 1914 the area was all broad-leaf woods, belonging at that time to the Earl of Mount Edgcumbe. During the war most of the trees were cut down and the wood used for the war effort. In 1918 service men were returning to the village and looking for work so these woods were then 'ripped' and the large tree roots removed. The plots were then let to the young men who set about planting the ground with bulbs and fruit in an attempt to make a living. Among those who rented these plots were Dick Cooper, Cecil Jane, Edward Rickard and Ern Duke."

As we continued our stroll we came across the remains of what had been Edward Rickard's stone packing house, the only recognisable part being the fireplace, the remainder was just a pile of rubble. Most of the original packing houses had open fire places where the women folk cooked food and dried wet clothing, as in busy times every daylight hour was spent in the market gardens and the sheds became a home from home.

Only the land on the left-hand side facing south had been cultivated, the opposite side had been mainly fruit trees and some old oak and sycamore had been retained. When the fruit trees died out, the National Trust, who by then were the custodians of the woodlands planted a number of fir trees and Courtney was one of those who took part in that project in the mid-1950s. The Trust now plants up all spare ground with conifers, which give a quick return as they mature much faster then the broad-leaf trees. They are then cut down and used mainly for papermaking. Courtney worked alongside other Trust workmen as they erected posts and wire netting around each new plantation

Picking 'Ornatus' at Sam Vospers, Woodlands: Dorothy Rickard, Lily Duke, Rhoda Striplin, Medlin, Avis Stephens, Edie Stephens, Win Olver. In the background are Sam Vosper, Albert Wadge, Bernard Martin, Arthur Martin and Marie. Note the strands of raffia for tying bunches. c.1926.

to keep out the rabbits, but as Courtney remarked to the Foreman at the time, "What about the rabbits you've trapped inside the fence!" That quip was typical of his sense of humour! Courtney recalled catching trout as a child in the deep parts of the stream, which runs through this land.

On returning to the road we then walked in the opposite direction along a track passed a field which Percy Symons had rented and on to the area described in George and Freda Brown's story which is related elsewhere in this book. On seeing this ground for the first time I could hardly believe that this was the same site that George and Freda had so carefully nurtured up until 1985. Everywhere fir trees towered 30 feet high or more and steps leading from the track up to the steep slopes of the gardens were barely discernible. We had no trouble finding George's stone-built packing house, as it is fully intact and has recently been renovated by the Trust. It is a well-built two-storey building, complete with chimney and could well have been a cottage. We climbed the stone steps along side and looked through the rear door on the second floor. We noticed the remains of a swallow's nest on the rafters and the Trust had obviously decided to use the shed for conservation purposes as they had erected a nesting box up in the eaves for Barn Owls. This may well be the last remaining stone packing shed of its type in the Cotehele valley and well worthy of preservation.

The whole area was very peaceful and the butterflies and dragonflies hovered around the ripening blackberries in the hedgerow. So different from the hive of activity it must have been a few years ago when the Brown's struggled against all odds to produce their first class crops. Freda told me on one of my visits to her, that she had never returned to the gardens since they had retired and I hope this description of the land she cultivated for so long will not upset her. It is now impossible to believe that these acres of fir trees and scrubland were once completely free of weeds.

If Freda and George and folk of their generation had not related their memoirs to me, soon no one would ever know just what the valley was like in the middle of this century. The land has gone full circle and returned once more to be as nature intended – a peaceful haven for wild life. This is typical of all the south slopes from Bartletts up past Cleave to Newton Farm, which when cultivated had provided a livelihood for so many villagers.

Few of the sons and daughters of the last generation of tenants are now prepared to work so hard in all weathers, in order to make a living and soon market gardens will be a thing of the past.

We left Boars Bridge and continued our nostalgic journey to Cotehele Bridge the entrance to the National Trust property, Cotehele House.

Facing us across the bridge was another plantation of fir trees, this time even more familiar to Courtney, for in the 1950s after farm labouring all day Courtney had spent the evenings 'ripping' this land by hand. Soon he was able to make a living here and he grew daffodils, strawberries, Iris and rhubarb amongst the pittosporum which provided him with an income in the winter months. It was from the banks of the river here at Cotehele Quay that Courtney spent many hours salmon fishing from a boat accompanied by Charlie, Bill and Viv Nelson.

In the 1960s he took over four acres of flat land in a field at Pitt Meadow. Stan Sleep rented the remainder of the field from the Trust. Here Courtney and his wife Margaret worked all the daylight hours producing spring cabbage, lettuce, leeks, gooseberries, daffodils and anemones. Most of this produce was sold to the wholesalers Marquands at Notterbridge. By this time Courtney had purchased a T 20 Ferguson tractor and machinery which made the cultivating easier, but all the produce had to be hand picked of course and it is not much fun washing and trimming leeks with white frost on the ground.

"Everybody worked like us did in they days, nobody took any notice cos we'd never known anything else. Except for some winter periods when I worked for the Trust I've done market gardening all me life – but I've had enough of it now and I just keep the ground outside Roundy Cottage clean and I don't plant nothing" remarked Courtney.

As we sat on the bridge Courtney was reminded of how during the Second World War, the Earl of Mount Edgcumbe had allowed the local men to cut down some trees below East Down. These were taken up to Bohetherick where, opposite the site of the old cider house, the men had dug a trench with picks and shovels with the intention of making themselves an air raid shelter. The trench some 30 feet long and 9 feet wide was dug into a field and these poles were then placed across the top side-by-side and back-filled with the soil which had been excavated. The entrance was via the road hedge and an emergency exit had been left at the rear.

"Half of 'em never used the place but us did and Bill and Lizzie Roberts, Eve Balsom and Bob Mitchell and sometimes when it got a bit bad, Tom Johns would come up from Haye Coombe. Some of us spent a brave bit of time in there."

After leaving the site of the shelter we returned to the lane where Courtney's cottage stands. We continued down this lane past Terry and Margaret Mitchell's home Haye Coombe Cottage and soon my guide was reminiscing again. I was told that Tom Johns lived there during the war years and 'gardened' the field below the cottage. When he 'packed up' Roy and Margery Rickard worked the field, having given up their few acres at Brentswood near Halton Quay. The next tenant was Charlie Hall. He had been a soldier stationed at Smeaton Hill Army Camp and on his 'demob' he returned to the village and cultivated the field.

Terry Mitchell has the field now, but all signs of cultivation are obliterated and the field had recently been cut for hay. As we turned from this gateway we had another wonderful view of the Tamar beyond the land which is part of Bohetherick farm and until recently was cultivated by Ivan Cradick. In past times it had been three fields divided by hedges but these had been removed by Ivan to enable him to use tractors and machinery more effectively. All the land had obviously been well-cared for unlike the adjoining piece of ground towards Haye. Fred Mutton and his wife worked this section of the valley for many years, but it is now a fir plantation with little to show of its past history. Their chicken house can still be seen but the remains of their packing shed is overgrown with ivy. Fred used to push all his produce on a wheelbarrow from this shed up the hill past Haye Coombe and Roundy Cottage to Bohetherick. From there Fred Rogers's lorry would collect the packages and transport them to Saltash railway station.

Alongside Fred Mutton's derelict garden is the site of the sewage works, which serves the whole parish.

Said Courtney "Some chap was down here one time and 'ee told me, 'you cud drink the water that comes out of there' so I said to 'en 'you have the first cupful and I'll have the second' but 'ee didn't do it you know."

So we didn't linger at the sewage works that day!

Now we had come to end of our tour. "You can ask Tommy Gorman 'bout Fursdon and Foxy Park, 'ee do know more 'bout that area then I do, and Alwyne Rickard will tell 'ee all the tale 'bout East Down and the Trenances", Courtney assured me.

So we returned to Roundy Cottage to recuperate. His fund of information exhausted, Courtney slumped into his chair and his thoughts turned to more important tasks.

"Now, what be I gain to get fur me tay?"

I left Courtney to produce his culinary delights; my own mind filled with a feast of facts, which I knew, would take me a long time to inwardly digest!

GROWERS IN COTEHELE VALLEY DURING HEIGHT OF ITS PRODUCTIVITY

Viv Nelson
J. Hoskin
P. Symons
W. Crowell
M. Crowell
W. Lee
Jack Langsford
E. Walsh
G. Gale
Gerald Langsford
Eric Rickard
Len Hughes
L. Babb
George Rickard
Sid Congdon
W. Congdon
Arthur Rabbage
Edward Vanstone
Ed Gale
Arnold Jope

G. Jope
J. Snell
Sid Tink
Frank Rogers
Frank Brown
G. Brown
W. Downing
W. Bond
Luke Hocking
Joe Snell
George Snell
G. Jackson
W. Broom
Edward Rickard
    (Comfort Wood)
Cecil Jane
    (Comfort Wood)
Dick Cooper
    (Comfort Wood)

Ben Vanstone. c.1920s.

CHAPTER SIX

Although it was the discovery of Joseph Snell's diaries that first aroused my interest, it has to be said that Joe was not the only 'Samuel Pepys' in St Dominick. Surprisingly when I began researching material for this book, the very first market gardener I approached was also a keen diarist. But George Brown's diaries differed from those of Joe's as they dealt solely with the everyday work pattern of his market garden. There was no mention of births, deaths or family matters in George's diaries; his was obviously kept as a record of when each particular crop was planted and harvested and when spraying and soil injection was carried out.

There was mention of vine weevil attack, crown rot, mildew, red spider mite, botrylis and verticillium wilt. Benlate, Tedion, Dimethoate, Vengar, Gramoxone, Ramrod, Rogor and Elvaron were the treatments sprayed on crops over the years with varying results.

On 22nd April 1977 the record read:

> **'Sprayed cabbage with high nitrogen liquid feed to counteract suspected deficiency, later was informed from Ellbridge (Experimental Station) trouble was more likely to be Manganese deficiency so sprayed with Epsom salts at 1lb per gallon, to run off ...'**

There was always an ongoing battle against pests and diseases. Indeed the introduction of pesticides, fungicides and weed killers was the most noticeable difference between the life-style of a market gardener in the 1960s and that of Joe Snell in the 1920s and 30s. The same weather conditions, fluctuating prices, successes and failures were faced by all the stalwart men and women who dedicated their lives to the production of fruit and vegetables and flowers during what must have been the Tamar Valley's most productive period ever – the 20th century. It was not a job for the faint hearted.

George and his wife spent their working lives on one of the steepest sites in the parish. Their land near Cotehele was on a one-in-four slope and they literally faced an up hill battle to stop the soil and produce from sliding down into the stream below!

But George, though small in stature, ('I was the baby of the family and the others kept patting me on the head – that's why I never grew very tall' joked George) never let the almost mountainous land around him, dwarf his spirit, even if the storms did on one occasion destroy his crops overnight. But that is George's story – I'll let him tell his tale in his own cheery way, with a little assistance from his hard-working wife and partner – Freda.

Boars Bridge

by George Brown

My name is George Brown and I was born in this house in Vogus Lane on 17th September 1919. I was the youngest child of Frank and Gertie Brown (*née* Lee) and my two sisters were Elsie and Winnie. Winnie is still around and lives in Callington.

We lived in this cottage until about 1923, but it wasn't called Gilfrege at that time and it was tied to Radland Farm where my father worked for Bessie Congdon. When he had to leave, we went to Jubilee Cottages near Halton Quay and lived with my mother's parents for three years. When the new Council houses were built at Tamar View we moved into the first one to be completed and remained there until 1931, then we went to a cottage adjoining Eastcott Farm, which Jim Reep owned. Father worked two acres at Eastcott and kept a field near the Butcher's Arms Public House.

I've moved around the village quite a bit over the years because we left Eastcott in September 1936 and went to live in one of a pair of nice big houses at Mount Pleasant, which was part of the Pentillie Estate.

Our neighbour was Heber Johns and they had four sons, Bill, Alfie, Ron and Tom and three daughters. Like father they worked a small farm and a few acres of market garden on steep ground across the valley from Crocadon Woods where they grew daffodils, tree fruit and vegetables.

We also worked the narrow strip of land on the opposite side of the road – land that was at one time, intended to be used as part of a railway link between St Dominick and Kelly Bray. Some of this land was taken over by Highways in 1997 when the road was widened, but daffodils still come into flower in the hedges there every spring.

My wife Freda is a few months younger than I am and her parents were market gardeners at Botus Fleming. Her grandfather, William Summerfield planted many of the cherry trees for which that village was famous.

We married in 1941 and our daughter Jill was born at Mount Pleasant in 1942.

Freda learnt to drive our Jowett van (Reg. No. DJY 49) and she still remembers the times she used to collect Myrtle Northcote and some other ladies in the village and drive them to the Trinity Chapel Sunday school for WI meetings. The passengers had to sit on chairs in the back

Freda Brown with Jowett van at Mount Pleasant. c.1945.

– it would never be allowed these days – and on one occasion Freda pulled up a bit sharp and when she looked around all she could see was Myrtle's feet up in the air – the chairs had all tumbled over!

When Jill was a baby we used to wheel her pram towards Vernigo, then we had to carry it down the steep stony track to the bottom of our market garden, where she would stay all day with Freda. We then reversed the operation at the end of the day and this would go on all through the busy season.

When Jill was about ten, Freda and I moved into the first of the new Council houses at Trehill Cross. The big ones were built before the war, but the remainder were not completed until 1952. By this time I had decided that farming was not for me – I didn't like the seven day week commitment that dairy work required. I preferred to work harder for six days and then have a day off, so I concentrated on the market garden side.

We had a small field on the left hand side of Halton road by Post Box (the cross roads situated a few yards from Mount Pleasant). In 1954 we moved back to this house and I came back to my roots. We worked Post Box field and I did casual work for various people. Then in the early 60s, George Rickard retired and we took over his couple of acres of garden at Boars Bridge in the Cleave Valley. These gardens stretched from Cotehele Quay to Watergate and was split up into some 20 holdings of a few acres each, all worked by different families. I can list the names of some of the tenants that were there around that period.

As time went on we took over adjacent sites as they became available and ended up working five and a half acres of extremely steep ground. There was a stone-built shed on our site where casual fruit pickers used to live in the 20s and 30s. These workers would travel from places like Gunnislake, Linkinhorne and other outlying villages, sleep all the week in the sheds and only travel home at the weekends. Freda used to take all our daily supply of food and water to the shed and prepare our meals on a Calor gas stove every day.

We grew spring flowers, spring cabbage, lettuce, strawberries, anemones and violets. The work was very labour intensive and in the early days we either dug the ground by hand or used the well tested method of pulling a plough up the steep incline by means of a wire rope attached to a winch situated at the top of the hill. I worked the plough and Freda manned the winch and it was very hard work, but we were used to it and had never known anything different. We used the same equipment to draw up earth too, using a large scoop. When anything needed moving from one area to another we commandeered sheets of old galvanise which we loaded with bags of bulbs and manure and we pulled these along with ropes.

In the 1970s we began to use the services of three local contractors. Geoff Martin, Roy Battershill and Michael Searle all did work for us at various times. Geoff had diggers, tractors and trailers which were useful when we wanted some excavating done in preparation for building a block wall and Michael and Roy did rotovating and earth moving for us which was a great improvement on our old fashioned method.

We rented our land from the National Trust, but originally it was part of the Mount Edgcumbe Estate. Our three gardens were known as Hearn's Wood, Brake and Boars Bridge. We were fortunate to have a stream running below our land and we had an agreement with Cornwall River Authority allowing us to extract water from the stream in times of need. The licence fee was £5 and this allowed us to extract up to 120,000 gallons. We pumped a supply to a storage tank and irrigated ground prior to planting crops or during prolonged periods of dry weather. For example in September 1978 we extracted water on 12 occasions for four hours a day at the rate of 6,000 gallons a day. The stream was a lifesaver at times.

Being situated in the Tamar Valley meant that our crops were ready early in the season and the big multiples wanted everything we could supply, but once fruit was available from Lincolnshire or Pembrokeshire, they didn't want ours as it was past its peak. That meant we had to find local markets for our fruit as the season progressed.

A market stall holder called Percy Dawe then came and collected directly from us and he used to take our carefully packed fruit and toss them in a heap, loose, on his stall, much to our dismay!

In the early days we sold our produce to Plymouth market and Fred Rogers collected it from the roadside by Newhouses, but in January 1968 we joined a Tamar Valley marketing project. Its full name was Tamar Valley and Elburton Growers Limited and we even had a brand name so that the groups produce could be recognised everywhere. This was STARPACK and the star sign was printed on all our boxes. Joining the group was good for us, as all we had to do was to grow the produce to the best of our ability. Although the prices were not always top-rate, the group took 100% of our produce, collected from the gate, took control of grading and selling and were very reliable.

They sold to Marks & Spencer and a quality control officer would come to the gardens and inspect our strawberries and they took nothing but the best for their stores. They insisted that the fruit be ripe all over when picked, as they were concerned about the appearance from the customer's point of view. Previously we had always picked when the tip of the strawberry was still white, but they wouldn't accept any white tipped fruit – they had to be perfection. However, later, they conceded that we and other growers were right to pick slightly under ripe fruit, as they travelled better. We grew the variety 'Favourite' and these were always popular with buyers representing Marks & Spencer.

In September 1975 we lost acres of strawberry plants due to an infestation of vine weevil. These small cream grubs feed on the roots of plants and the plants suddenly wilt and die. We had to spray them with DDT and this meant filling our water tank, which was at the top of the slope, with a mixture consisting of half a pint concentrate to 100 gallons of water. It was Freda's job to keep the tank topped up, whilst I went down every row with a three-quarter inch hosepipe drenching the plants. It did the trick and we didn't have vine weevil again. However, DDT is banned now and other brand names have been introduced that hopefully aren't so harmful to other wild life and humans.

We planted new 'maiden' plants every year and ripped up the two-year-old beds and burnt them, so that prevented too many pests and viruses infecting our crops.

George and Freda Brown at work on their steep holding at Boars Bridge. Courtesy of 'Grower Nexus Horticulture'. c.1983.

We had to use a lot of pesticides and fungicides for different crops at various times of the year and also weed suppressants too – everyone did.

We also suffered frost damage at times, one year we had a beautiful bed of lettuce and they caught the frost and we didn't cut one. We had our failures and disappointments, but we think our biggest heartbreak was caused by a severe storm. This was on the night of July 6th–7th 1975. There was a violent thunderstorm, worst in living memory. The sky was a strange pink colour, it was weird and the rain was horrendous. Freda was afraid to go to bed and we sat up all night and when we went to work the next morning a terrible sight met our eyes. The heavy rain had taken about 150 tons of top soil from three recently injected plots, one of which had been planted up a week or so previously with anemone corms, and deposited the lot down the bottom of our steep garden. Young strawberry runners, which were growing on for the next season, were ripped off the mother plants and washed out of the ground and covered in mud. We were devastated, but we had to pull ourselves together and try to rescue what we could. I used a heavy rake to fill in some of the deep channels caused by the rushing water and pushed the runners back into the soil and put a stone on each one to give them a chance to re-root. The next day Michael Searle arrived with his machinery and over the next few days, between heavy showers of rain, we got the soil into a trailer and took load after load around the road. We deposited it at the top of the field and then rotovated it into some semblance of tilth and looking less like a battlefield. During this time Freda and I picked up literally thousands of anemone corms that were just sprouting – we had buckets full and all of them had to be replanted after the soil was prepared and manured again. All in all it was a very difficult job even with the help of mechanical aids and that storm was very costly for us.

Another time, I had a lucky escape in a tractor incident. I'd cut down some old apple trees down the bottom of the hill and I rigged up a wire rope system attached to my tractor at the top. I dragged each tree to the top, then I reversed the tractor a bit to slacken the rope so that I could unhitch it, before taking the rope to the bottom again, to repeat the procedure. I'd nearly finished the job and I'd reversed the tractor a bit and was undoing the rope to use again when I glanced up and saw the tractor moving slowly across the piece of ground. I rushed over to try and stop it and just as I reached the back wheels the whole thing tipped over. Luckily I was above the tractor and so was

George Brown planting Valdor lettuce. Note the 'wrapper' apron made from an old sack, which was normal wet weather attire. Courtesy of 'Grower Nexus Horticulture'. c.1983.

Freda Brown picking St Piran anemones. Courtesy of 'Grower Nexus Horticulture'. c.1983.

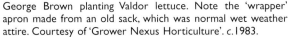

not knocked over, but it rolled all the way from the top to the bottom and was a complete wreck. If I had been one tick earlier I'd have been on that tractor and I'd have been killed. It wasn't funny to see it all smashed up, but I was lucky to be alive.

And so our days were spent: cleaning ground, planting young plants, seeds, bulbs and corms, manuring, spraying, watering and harvesting. Often Freda would be bunching anemones till midnight to ensure they were ready for next day's market. It was a hard life but very satisfying.

But it wasn't all work; we had some interesting outings during the period that the Ellbridge Experimental Station was in existence. This body was set up to give advice and information to Tamar Valley growers and we used their services on numerous occasions. Dan DuPlessis from Landulph is an expert in the cultivation of daffodils and was very much involved with Ellbridge. M.A.F.F. (Ministry of Agriculture Fisheries and Food) Officers organised trips to various market gardens and places of interest and we often went along. It was a good day out.

One such outing during May was to a strawberry producing area in Cheddar where we were interested to see young girls laying chopped straw beneath the plants to protect the fruit, something we never did down this way. The chopped straw was very sharp so the girls wore gauntlet gloves to protect their hands and arms. I also recall an outing to see the anemone fields – acres of bright flowers in full bloom, an unusual sight for us, as anemones for market are always picked in bud, but these were being grown for seed. On that occasion, because we had travelled from another area, we had to walk through a trough of disinfectant to ensure we brought no diseases on to the land.

The Experimental Station at Ellbridge, near Saltash, was of great assistance to the local growers as experts were always available to give advice on any problems we encountered. Ellbridge and Roswarne in West Cornwall were under the same command and when, sadly, Ellbridge was forced to close down in 1974 for economic reasons Mike Pollock, who had become a friend as well as an adviser to us over the years, became director of Rosewarne. We often travelled down there for various lectures and demonstrations. These visits were also returned, as in 1971 and 72 we entertained groups of growers from Cheddar and they were amazed to see how we managed to produce crops on land they would consider impossible to work. We have letters from Mike Pollock the Horticultural Advising Officer and C M Green the Divisional Officer of A.D.A.S. thanking us for allowing the groups to visit us.

Ellbridge Experimental Station

Ellbridge Experimental Station was opened by he Council in 1927 and taken over by the Ministry of Agriculture in 1945. There were three such establishments in the Cornwall region, the others being at Rosewarne in West Cornwall and on the Isles of Scilly. Ellbridge consisted of five acres of land, which was used for experimental purposes and advisors were always on call to assist growers in the Tamar Valley. In the early days, there were an estimated 15,000 producers growing various crops in the whole valley, but by the mid-60s this had reduced to around 160 registered growers. Now, at the turn of the century, those working land commercially would probably be in the region of 25. The closure to freight on the Calstock rail line in 1961, meant growers lost a vital link to upcountry markets and thus began the rapid decline in the era of market gardening in the Tamar Valley. The Ellbridge Experimental Station closed in 1974 for economic reasons.
For those interested in the history of horticulture, a booklet entitled 'Horticulture in the Tamar Valley' by Mike Pollock (ex-advisor at Ellbridge) would make valuable reading.

Information courtesy of Richard Harnett of Kernow Nurseries Pillaton.

One such letter from Stephen Salter, the then Horticultural Adviser for M.A.F.F. stated,
'I think without exception, the growers were absolutely staggered at how you grew first rate crops on land they would consider impossible to work. I must say that by the time I had reached the top of your slope, I was just about 'finished' for the day. I think you must be the fittest man in the whole of the Tamar Valley!'

Freda and I had a few moments of glory, when we were featured in the 'Commercial Grower' in June 1964, when we shared an interview and photographs with Albert Wills from Strawberry Hill. Despite its name, Strawberry Hill is relatively flat and I think the two gardens were chosen to show the comparisons.

In 1979 we were again in the limelight when we featured in 'The Field', along with Dan DuPlessis and Gerald Veale.

Then in December 1983 a year before we retired, we had a write up and more photographs in an issue of 'Grower' which stated,
'Take five and a half acres with six inches of topsoil, stand it on end, face them due south in the Tamar Valley. Add a rough track, a reliable stream at the bottom and 100 yards up at the top

of the garden put a narrow road for access. Fence the whole plot with netting to keep the rabbits out. Now make yourself a living' – This just about described our land and we did make a living!

Although I do not have any particular hobby, except my allotment up by the school, Freda still keeps up her interest in singing. She loves singing and in 1965 she joined the newly formed group of locals known as 'The Dominiques'. Although the group was only available for concerts during the less busy periods in the gardening calendar, they quickly became very popular and have travelled all over Devon and Cornwall. The group consists of husband and wife Jean and Bert Laing, Freda and our daughter Jill on piano.

It all began in 1965 when they got together and decided to enter a talent contest at Liskeard, which they won and their prize was a holiday at Butlins in Bognor Regis. They did three shows there and entertained 7,000 people in all and once again they won the competition which was another holiday which they enjoyed the following August.

They all attend Chapel, so most of their concerts were held in Chapels and they have sung at Lanivet, Summercourt, Hayle and Trispen and practically every village in between. Their fame spread across the Tamar, and as far away as Hartland and Barnstaple – they travelled miles. Sometimes Terry Rogers went along to act as compere and they sang a very varied selection of music. They enjoyed singing well known tuneful songs like 'Jimmy Brown' and 'I Believe' and their concerts were always well supported. Freda also recites and tells 'yarns' and is a very confident entertainer. They still do the occasional concert and a few weeks ago the preacher at Ebenezer Chapel, which Freda attends, came from Bradworthy and he remembered well the concert they performed up there years ago.

We have some good memories to look back on now that we are not quite as able as we used to be. We spend a lot of time sitting in our conservatory which has a wonderful view across country and we watch the aeroplanes from Plymouth airport as they fly to far-off places, but we do not envy them. We have had a very happy life together and are content with our quiet lives here in our home at St Dominick.

1919

Jan 10	Jack Matthews spoke of his disgraceful wage.		Aug 23	Market a 'drag' came back to Saltash Races.
Jan 31	Planted fig trees.		Aug 27	W.Coryton died.
Feb 4	Went to meeting to decide what form of memorial to erect for our boys who have fallen in the war.		Sept 10	Miss F.Downing married.
			Sept 27	Great railway strike.
			Sept 28	Two faces of Church clock fixed.
Feb 10	E Duke came to work first time after the war.		Oct 3	Many strangers to meet steamer owing to Railway strike.
Mar 5	Transplanted michaelmas daisies and A Jope took 40 acres of Eastcott.		Oct 21	Miss Martin Jubilee married to Mr Waye.
Mar 8	First three bunches of rhubarb for market.		Nov 3	A J received summons for not having his dog muzzled.
Mar 28	Raised Jack's wage to 28/- a week.		Nov 14	Bartlett's hill a sheet of ice.
June 1	A J and I went our annual fruit garden trip.		Nov 15	Drove to market with roads like glass bottle.
July 29	Henry Collins married.		Dec 9	Went to dance. Danced Maxina, one-step and Military 3 step 1st time
Aug 14	Picked 25,000 beans.4,200 acres Quithiock Estate sold (Pentillie).		Dec 23	May Forest played for our dance class 1st time and Jack Batten's accordine. *(Accordion).*
Aug 15	Beans 8/- thousand. Plums 8/- dozen pounds at market.			

St Dominick Church School

Back row: ?, Alec Cradick, George Jope, Jack Taylor, Harold Maunder, Raymond Martin. *Middle row*: William Langsford, Phyllis Jope, ?, Mary Smith, ? Hambridge, Joyce Congdon, Thelma Cobbledick, Lorna ?, Doris Jope, Joyce Langsford, Florrie Taylor, Douglas Martin. *Front row*: ?, Jim Maunder, Phyllis Duke, Mildred Rosekilly, Betty Martin, Audrey Worth, ?, Donald Jane. *c*.1933.

St. Dominick School

Back row Miss Bath (teacher), Barbara Crocker (Striplin), Alwyne Rickard, Donald Borlase, Marion Herring (Rogers). *Middle row*: Joyce Collins (Veale), Jean Strike, Sheila Strike, Pauline Langsford, Joyce Rickard. *Front row*: Courtney Vanstone, Max O'Dowd, Valerie Duke (Kellow), Jean Rickard (Laing), Raymond Duke, Jim Dawe. *c*. late 1930s.

CHAPTER SEVEN

There had been a market at Devonport since the 1760s, but the 'new' market was built in 1852 at a cost of £2,000. It was kept well supplied with produce grown on land near the Tamar and Tavy rivers, which was then transported by the steamer Empress, which plied between Calstock and North Corner at Devonport, on Tuesdays, Thursdays and Saturdays.

More often than not, it was the womenfolk who made these early morning trips. Horse-drawn vehicles, laden with seasonal produce took them to the nearest port of call. The men would see everything safely on board and then return to their work, leaving the women to chat amongst themselves on the long journey down river. But with gossip to exchange over hot mugs of tea in the cabin below deck, the time soon passed. When the steamer docked at North Corner, they had to carry their heavy baskets of eggs, butter, flowers, fruit and vegetables, along the cobbled street to the market place at Devonport.

Carriers with horse and wagon waited at the dockside to assist with the transportation of bulky boxes and containers from the steamer to the market. The stalls were filled with the fresh goods and the ladies then spent the day selling their wares.

The market was a noisy, cheerful place with all manner of things for sale other than the garden and farm produce. After the food traders left at four-o-clock to catch the steamer for their return trip, the 'cheap jacks' would take over the stalls. Their cheeky banter and bargain goods meant the market did not close until ten-o-clock at night.

During the Second World War, part of the market and many Devonport shops were destroyed by enemy action and Devonport Market never really recovered from the onslaught. Over the next few years parts of the old market area were taken over by the Dockyard. Much of the structure still stands inside the Dockyard walls, and it is a listed building. The last wholesalers, E Marquand & Co. left Devonport in 1961.

During the war, Plymouth Market consisted of rows of outdoor stalls and became known as Tin Pan Alley, the main market building having been commandeered by the large chain stores when their original buildings were blitzed. The old Plymouth market closed at the end of August 1959 and was replaced by the present market at Frankfort Gate. This market was opened on 7th September 1959, and the old market was demolished and replaced by new stores.

The Morrishes and the Markets

by Jim Morrish

I am William James Morrish and I was born 76 years ago. I was named after my two grandfathers. My paternal grandfather was William Morrish of Saltash and my mother Mable's father, was James Rabbage of St.Dominick. I had aunts and uncles in the village and I spent a lot of time during the school holidays, with my aunt Ethel Ford who kept the Post Office. I used to sleep in the room above the shop. My grandparents and parents always had a stall in Devonport market, which in the early days was situated within easy reach of the steamers, which took local produce from the Tamar Valley to be sold there. Around the mid-1930s, due mainly to the more general use of motor vehicles the steamer trade died down and the market moved into Plymouth and was sited roughly in the area of where the Marks & Spencer store is today. My father was one of the last to use a horse and cart to travel from Saltash across the Ferry and on into Plymouth market. He stabled his horse up by the old sugar refinery behind George Street Chapel, in those days.

When Plymouth was blitzed during 1941, Marks & Spencer and Woolworth's took over a large part of the covered market, which meant the smaller stall holders were obliged to set up their pitches outdoors in what became known as Tin Pan Alley. Around this period my family started selling wholesale off a lorry alongside the market, but Mother always kept a small stall inside the

Tin Pan Alley

This temporary market was set up outside the original Plymouth Market and was familiar to local growers, who regularly set-up their stalls there during and after the War. The market building was commandeered by the large chain stores after their premises were destroyed by enemy action. The market closed in 1959 when a new market was built at Frankfort Gate. c.1946.

Courtesy of *Western Evening Herald.*

market under the stairs. Most local market gardeners sold their produce at this market, or in later years at the new site created when Plymouth was rebuilt after the war.

Joe Snell and his sister, Alice, had worked about 18 acres in the Radland Valley since 1914 and grew a vast selection of fruit, flowers and vegetables. The bulk of the daffodils and fruit were sent by rail to markets up country during the peak seasons, but a lot of produce was taken to Plymouth market during the remainder of the year. Joe always had something to sell all year round as he grew such varied crops and did not rely on daffodils, cherries and strawberries for his main source of income, as many local growers did. Joe took goods to market in his own Ford lorry in later years, but previously he used the services of Jack Taylor's covered lorry. Jack Taylor erected a garage for his lorry on flat land belonging to Joe, just inside Whitegate on the Berry Road, as there was no space for a garage alongside his cottage home by Radland Mill.

Joe's ground consisted of over twenty different plots, most of which were cultivated, but he had orchards and a pond which, in early days, had fed the corn mill, which closed down in the last century. His gardens stretched below Berry Road from Whitegate (this entrance is a public footpath and a bridleway), almost to the entrance to Higher Berry Farm. He had four separate pieces in that particular area, the first was known as Watergate, the next was Pond Field, then came Middlepiece, where Joe erected his greenhouse in 1918 and finally Higher Field. Ground beyond this was owned and worked by Arnold Jope of Higher Berry Farm. There were also areas of pasture where Joe kept poultry and a cow. It has all gone back to scrub and woodland now and it is hard to believe that 35 years ago the ground was fully productive.

My family's land was at Pill in Saltash, but of course I knew the Snells all my life, because they had a stall near my mother's and I have been a regular visitor to the market since I was four years old!

Joe's other sister Mary, tended Snell's stall and she was married to Ernest Duke and their only child Phyllis often accompanied her family to market and Phyllis and I got to know each other well over the years. I did my courting in Plymouth market!

Joe Snell understood every aspect of market gardening and grew fruit and vegetables of every description. He was very interested in the art of producing new varieties of daffodils. He spent years cross-pollinating different daffodils, sowing the seed and then waiting patiently for the seedlings to grow into flower producing bulbs. We discovered after his death, that all his experiments were carefully logged in his diaries. He could often be seen in his greenhouse at night when he knew that a particular flower was just at the right stage to be pollinated by hand. Joe did not rely on the bees to do this work for him despite the fact that his property included a rare bee house which, incidentally, has recently been restored. Joe never registered his new varieties, but was offered £500 on one occasion when he produced a particularly good specimen which he named Rich Cup. Joe wished to increase the stock of the bulb himself, but sadly he died suddenly before he achieved his aim and I fear his new daffodils disappeared without trace. It is quite possible that they might well be thriving in the valley somewhere, despite the lapse of time, as many of his daffodils do appear in the woods each spring without any attention having been given to them.

Joe grew many cherries in the valley and planted gribbles which he later grafted with a suitable variety with his old stock and the valley was a wonderful sight in April when the blossom was in full bloom. He had apples, pears and figs, Early River, Czar and Victoria plums, also damsons, strawberries and all types of soft fruit. He bought his punnets and chip baskets from Fred Rogers's store at Pitt Meadow and his ladders were made by Richard Striplin in Baber Lane. These were stored on racks behind his cottage in winter months. In the area known as Pond Field, he grew scores of Czar plum trees and I remember picking them many a time using the 28 or 35 bar ladders, but I never ventured up the 54 bar ladder he owned! He employed two brothers on a regular basis, Ward and Jack Matthews who lived out Metherell way. Their family was very musical and gave concerts all around the district.

Joe's sisters Alice and Mary also worked on the ground and at cherry time he employed a number of workers on a casual basis. Joe also kept a couple of cows and sold cream and butter when there was a surplus. He kept pigs and killed two or three a week all through autumn and winter. He sold them to butcher Jim Reep or took them to market along with hogs puddings, liver and tripe. He always had eggs for market and sat a lot of broody hens every spring to bring on fresh stock, the older hens were then killed off and sold as pie fowls.

Joe was a regular church goer and was very fond of sport, he supported the local football team and went to boxing matches and taught the young Taylor boys to box. He regularly went hare coursing on Viverdon Downs, taught himself to swim, attended concerts and other fund-raising activities in the village and was always interested in national affairs. Sadly in the autumn of 1938, Joe Snell was accidentally killed when he was thrown out of a moving Western National bus at Vernigo cross-roads. After his death Alice continued to live at their little cottage, the family pulled together and with the help of Ned Cole, kept the market garden going. Alice was a quiet lady, many thought her eccentric, but she was a dear soul and straight-as-a-die.

During 1952 my parents gave up their ground at Saltash so I was then available to help out too and we worked there until Alice's death in 1965. In 1947 Phyllis and I had married and we lived at Little Smeaton. There was a field of about four acres surrounding the house and we worked that and Radland together. After Alice's death the land and cottage was left to Joe's brother Benjamin, who had left the area and moved to Trematon many years before. He was not interested in market gardening and soon put the place up for sale, so Phyllis and I began to work our own piece of land at Smeaton more intensively. We put up greenhouses over the years and grew tomatoes and chrysanths and Phyllis began to grow annual bedding plants. As time went on this side of the business grew to become our main source of income. Phyllis grew the plants from seed and did most of the pricking out and tending of the thousands of seedlings.

I still continued to visit the market twice a week and some local growers began to bring their produce to me for sale in Plymouth. By this time, I had built up a trade calling on various shops in and around Plymouth. They took our tomatoes, runner beans, sweet peas and chrysanths and also most of the bedding plants. We supply Reg Collins at St Budeaux, 'Bloomin' Lovely' at Higher St Budeaux the Lynher Stores at Weston Mill and Triffords in Wolsely Road. My son Brian has taken over the market trips now and he still does a similar round carrying on where I left off. Our daughter Diana helps us out too, so we are a family concern.

In Alice Snell's latter years her cottage became very dilapidated and a year or two after her death it was condemned as no one had lived in it since 1965. An outsider had purchased the cottage from Ben Snell and in 1967 the place became notorious, as it was featured in the *News of the World*! This gentleman was a property dealer and he had

'BUS PASSENGER KILLED

St. Dominick Man Involved In St. Mellion Crash

VEHICLE DITCHED

The sole passenger was killed when a Western National 'bus was involved in an accident at Ryland's Cross, near St. Mellion, on its way from Callington to Saltash yesterday.

He was Joseph Snell, a market gardener, single, and aged about 50, of Radland Mill, St. Dominick, who, it appears, was thrown out when the 'bus apparently got into a ditch.

The vehicle finished with its near-side wheels in the ditch, its body against the hedge.

The driver was William Jackson, of Callington.

Report of Joe Snell's death which appeared in a local newspaper. P. C. Berryman attended the scene of the accident.
Courtesy of *Western Morning News*.

advertised the cottage and a few acres of the land for sale at £500. The advertisement appeared in between 150 and 200 publications and such was the interest shown he received 10,000 replies from prospective buyers! Apparently he was so overwhelmed, that he had thousands of letters printed which suggested that the demolition order on the cottage had every chance of being rescinded and asking for £1 from anyone who wanted more explicit information. Unfortunately for him, his little money making scheme was discovered before he could pocket much of the cash, but he was taken to Court and faced eleven charges of attempting to obtain £1 by falsely pretending the demolition order was not final. He was found not guilty and discharged – his rather appropriate name was Mr Connor! Yet more interest was aroused when the new owner of Snell's land offered plots of land for sale at £25 each, on which buyers were assured they could erect a holiday chalet if they so wished. This too proved to be a con and a few people were very disappointed when they discovered they had handed over cash for plots of rough woodland, with no hopes of planning permission being granted.

Lately the land has been allowed to return to nature. Joe's cottage has been demolished and only his pig and cow houses now remain. His other shed and the historic bee house have been restored, but as yet no one has obtained planning permission to rebuild Joe's old home. The cottage where the Taylor family lived has long since fallen down and only the mill remains habitable. Its latest owners are Julian Cradick and his wife and children – a local family – who live a secluded life in this now deeply wooded valley, with only the arrival each spring of the few remaining daffodils to remind them of the thriving business which was once carried on in the hamlet of Radland Mill.

Joe's apple and pear trees have probably died of old age and neglect and when I look back I recall that every farmer had an orchard alongside their property. I know that Bill Martin at Heathfield had orchards sweeping down towards Crocadon Woods and some of his trees are still fruitful. He also grew acres of cabbage plants and supplied the whole district. Practically everyone I know went to Heathfield for their plants.

Phyllis and I still carry on with some work in the field and greenhouses especially the bedding plants and chrysanths, which Phyllis bunches for our son Brian to take to market twice a week. She also makes scores of Holly wreaths at Christmas time. For years she made all the funeral wreaths in the Parish and like her Uncle Joe she has a record of them all, so knows the date of the demise of almost everyone in the village over the years. She likes to keep things for sentimental reasons and I am always getting into trouble for disposing of bits and pieces that she thinks should be kept. I must admit she probably has the right idea, as these items of information are useful when someone wants to record the History of the Village!

1920

Jan 29	Went to J D Langsford's for straw.
Feb 13	Grafted 2 cherries by lake Burcome (*Burcombe*) and Bulyn (*Bullion*).
Mar 21	Went to Comfort Wood lovely day and plum blossom in full bloom.
May 13	A.Jope's 36th birthday.
June 26	Had sea bath 1st for year.
July 25	Meet W.Congdon and 'Elloner' (*Eleanor*) after church 1st time.
Aug 13	Mrs.W.Congdon a daughter.
Aug 27	A.J. accident ran over 3 year old boy in King Street Plymouth and killed him.
Aug 28	A.J. at market much upset.
Sept 10	Market with 46,000 beans 1/- per 1,000.
Sept 23	Knew that Ford motor-cars dropped to pre-war price.
Oct 21	Went Moss Side for 1,000 raspberry canes and A.J. family 1st. night at Eastcott and E Duke collected his 2,000 strawberry plants.
Oct 27	Took up 2,000 strawberry plants for Hoskin.
Oct 29	Took up 1,000 strawberry plants for Hoskin.
Oct 30	Took up 3,400 strawberry plants for Symons.
Nov 1	Took up 4,500 strawberry plants for Symons.
Nov 2	Took up 7,900 strawberry plants for Symons £1 per 1,000.
Nov 8	Went Hunt meet at Oak Tree.
Nov 10	Took up 5,000 strawberry plants for S.Perkins.
Nov 11	Drawing up earth all day. Stopped work for two minutes at 11am Armistice Day.
Nov 13	Eastcott sold to J. Reep.
Nov 22	Went Corneal threshing.
Nov 30	Threshing at Ashton and a very nice evening at dance class about 40 there.
Dec 5	Went to Comfort Wood and picked three primroses and G.Rickard wore trilby hat first time.
Dec 4	St.Dominick beat Kelly Bray 4 to 1.
Dec 7	A good lot at dance class but a little gloom with chaps owing to S.Mutton resenting not chosen to play football.
Dec 13	A very heavy fall of snow at Plymouth and white here and boys 'cracked' stone and 'pitched' potatoes.
Dec 16	Went coursing at Viverdon caught 8 and started 46 hare.
Dec 24	'Pitched' potatoes all day and went pub in evening.
Dec 25	Went Church morning and evening and Calstock beat St. Dominick 3 to 1.
Dec 30	Our 'long-night' dance a real good time.

1921

Apr 8	Eclipse of sun.
Apr 19	Went to Fred Rogers about ordering a motor car.
Apr 21	Went to tennis whist drive and dance, delightful time.
Apr 23	Bought motor car for first time.
Apr 23	Went to Metherell concert given by the Matthew's family – very good.
Apr 24	Cherry blossom at its best.
Apr 29	Drove car from Berry Gate to Watergate by myself.
May 8	Size in boots 8, size in collars 15½, size in hats 6½, weight 11st 10lb. Height 5 ft 6½in.
May 20	Man came with petrol 1st time. I had three cans (6 gallons) 3/1 per gallon.
May 23	Went to meeting to arrange about greeting the Prince.
May 24	Put in some cucumbers and the Prince stopped at school and shook hands with all our ex soldiers – the general opinion, a nice gentleman.
June 11	Bought timber for motor house.
June 16	Miss Moon helped us pick strawberries in evening.
June 18	P Jones and C Guest started cherry picking.
June 20	117 dozen cherries picked by 11 p.m.
June 23	120 Dozen cherries for market.
July 21	Our cricketers beat Botus Fleming and went Eastcott to see trotting match. Started to pick early plums.
July 27	Went to Kelly Bray with 170 chips of cherries.
Aug 5	Picked 40 dozen Czars (plums)
Aug 6	Finished cherry picking.
Aug 7	Bank holiday. Mary Snell and I went to the races.
Aug 15	Picked pears off tree by figs.
Aug 19	Picked blackberries for market.
Aug 30	Miss Lashbrook and Mr Veal married.
Sep 9	Last of damsons and 12lb of grapes for market.
Sep 28	Charlie Langsford rode down on his motor bike.
Sep 29	Mr G Martin Towell married Miss Alberta Langsford.
Oct 5	Frank Rogers's 1st trip with his motor car.
Oct 7	Frank Rogers goes to Devonport with marketing 1st time.
Dec 27	Matthews's family gave concert at Bere Alston.
Dec 28	George Rickard and Lucy Reep married.

Back row: Wendell Fry, Phyllis Rickard (Rickard), Marion Fry (Gibbs), Christine Hill (Gorman), Ernestine Herring (Cradick), Clifford Striplin. *Middle row*: Harry Martin, Jean Martin (Martin), Donald Striplin, Doris Collins (Shires), Betty Rickard (Feltham), Francis Wadge (King), Marion Herring (Rogers) Geoffrey Mason, Inez Olver (Martin). *Front row*: Gordon Strike, Jack Striplin, Peter Sleep, Stuart Martin, Donald Borlase, Ambrey Roberts. *c.* early 1930s.

CHAPTER EIGHT

Throughout my childhood I was familiar with the expression 'Maunders to Haye'. This was the way a particular branch of a family was recognised in those days, when large families meant the same surname being used by many households in the Parish. Including the name of a person's home, made them more easily identifiable especially when that family had lived and worked in one particular location for several generations. Although Haye Farm was a place I had often heard of, I had never had reason to visit it.

When I was researching material for 'A Stitch in Time', I interviewed Sid Mutton at Strip Haye Farm. I did not venture beyond Sid's house on that occasion and had no idea what lay ahead.

Recently, I contacted Peggy Kusiak and her daughter Jo during my quest for another family story and I was told that they had lived at Haye Farm for many years. I decided to venture down Haye Lane, to discover for myself the farm and the surrounding fields. Having first gained permission from the Hunn family, who presently rent the land, I set off accompanied by my husband, daughter and the family dog.

Haye Farm is situated a few yards beyond Strip Haye in Bohetherick. When we went there the house was unoccupied but under renovation. It belongs to the National Trust and is a typical farmhouse with a slate floored dairy and a pump and granite trough outside the back door. Its features include a cobbled yard, a mounting stone and a little walled garden. Had I been twenty years younger, I would have found it hard to resist the temptation to rescue such a charming farmhouse and renovate its neglected garden. We continued our walk past traditional barns, cow-chawls and a wagon house and into a lane that I had been told, would take me to the Jam House. Courtney Vanstone had pointed out this building from the opposite side of the valley, when we were at Woodlands and he had told me that jam was made there many years ago and the building was known by locals, as the Jam House. We travelled about half a mile down a narrow track until we reached a stone building on our right. We went into the field and examined it more closely. It was a small two-storey house, but now only part of the upper floor was still in place, with the remainder open to the roof. One gable-end, facing down river, was open to the elements and it was being used as a shelter for cattle, but an open fireplace and rounded chimneybreast was still intact in the far corner. Despite its isolation, it was quite feasible that this had, indeed, been used as a small jam factory, as its name suggests. Jo said her family always called it the apple house and that orchards surrounded the building till the middle of the century.

I had been keen to visit Jam House ever since it was first mentioned to me by villagers back in 1984, but finding proof of its original use was proving impossible. Not a jam jar or a 'Golly' label could I spy and the little house by the marshy banks of the River Tamar still holds on to its secret past.

As we returned to our car, we passed a stone shed at Strip Haye and I noticed smoke issuing from a metal chimney in the roof. I peered into the dark interior and to my surprise, I saw a farrier at work. He told me he was John Howie and that he had taken over the tenancy of Strip Haye on the death of the previous tenant, Sid Mutton. How satisfying it was to watch a young man at work at an anvil; red-hot embers glowing in the semi-darkness and that special smell associated with a blacksmith's shop. It was quite the most re-assuring thing I had seen on my journey around St. Dominick. Everywhere I had been before, I had heard tales of the changes in village life, but here was someone still practising the age-old craft of a farrier.

All is not lost!

I had many conversations with Jo and her mother over the next few weeks and Jo took me on another visit to Haye. On that occasion, she showed me the site of the mine Captain's house and the old lead and silver mine. Jo told me about the special steps, that were at one time set into the boundary hedge between Chaybel (Chapel) Farm and Haye and which were in daily use by the postman, as he travelled on his round between Chaybel Farm and Cotehele. I mentioned that my mother used to tell us that when the Bridgmans lived at Haye Farm in the late 1930s, tennis parties were held there. Jo was not aware of this, but we decided that the tennis court must have been in one of the fields behind the cow-chawles, but it was difficult to imagine a time when such genteel activities took place on a working farm. Tennis was a very popular pastime in the village at that period and a number of families had private tennis courts.

So many things that were general knowledge a generation or so ago, are now only memories in the minds of the few remaining people with local knowledge. One such person, Peggy Kusiak, will no doubt stir memories among the older generation, with her interpretation of 'The Maunders to Haye'.

Maunders to Haye

by Peggy Kusiak

I am Peggy Kusiak, *née* Maunder. I was born at Stockwell Farm in 1923 and my mother Dorothy, was one of thirteen children of the Langsford family from Cotehele Mill.

Natalie, you and I are related you know, as we both descended from Charles Langsford senior, who was our great-grandfather. My father was Harold Maunder and I had five brothers and sisters, Marjorie (Gregory), Harold junior, who married butcher Reep's daughter, Amy, and Jim who married Dorothy Tarr and now lives at Metherell. Then there was Dorothy (Lucas) and Kitty.

When my grandfather Charles junior retired from Cotehele Mill in 1914 and my uncle, Harold Langsford took over the milling business, Grandfather and his two daughters Mary and Kate moved to Stockwell and Grandfather died there.

During the First World War my father Harold Maunder and his brother-in-law, Arnold Martin were called up and their wives and Mary worked Stockwell Farm whilst they were away at war. On their return Uncle Arnold and Aunt Kate went to live at Lanreath and my father took over Stockwell.

I had a very happy childhood at Stockwell. We had lots of cousins and other relations and they were always coming to visit us, especially on Sunday mornings. The farm belonged to the Earl of Mount Edgcumbe at that time. There were plots of land up Stockwell Lane when I was a youngster, which were rented by different local people. I recall that my uncle Len Cradick, Tony and Ivan's grandfather, was one of the tenants. He lived in Baber Lane with his wife and four sons.

Bill Collins also made his living there, working a couple of acres of market garden. He lived in a small asbestos bungalow at the end of the lane. He always came to our farm every morning to collect some milk in a tiny jug. He had a terrier called Winky who usually accompanied him wherever he went. Bill visited us three times everyday except Sunday and usually arrived in time to hear the one-o-clock and six-o-clock news bulletins on our wireless. He stayed a while for a chat, then went off to the pub. That was his routine for years. On from Bill, was his stepbrother Henry Collins's field. He ran a threshing business, but he and his family kept the garden going as well, as threshing was mainly a seasonable job. During the war his daughter Doris helped too, along with her brother Fred. Joe Collins was too young at that time to do much, but he too, kept some ground in later life. William Friendship worked land at Stockwell in conjunction with his threshing business. Then came Mr Jennings who lived down Burraton Green. He was quite up to date as he had a greenhouse in his cottage garden! Across the lane, Jim Hill had some land, then came Mrs Finch; she was the widowed mother of George Finch. There were always people travelling up and down the lane in those days as they went to and from work. A public well was situated in Stockwell and people from nearby cottages had to come there to collect their drinking water, prior to the installation of a mains water supply in the 1930s. I loved seeing all the activity. The well has been filled in now and some of the hedges have been destroyed, it is not like it was when we were children.

When Mr Bridgeman left Haye Farm in 1940, my father took it over, as by then he had two grown up sons and Stockwell was only a small farm. My father and brothers, Harold and Jim ran both farms till Jim married, then he and his wife lived at Stockwell.

When we were youngsters we used to play in a derelict house on Haye mash with our cousins the Cradick boys, who had, by this time, moved to Greenbank Farm. I have been told the old house was once a mine Captain's house and it was situated at the end of the lane below the Jam House. It is still possible to see the raised track across the mash, which led to the river bank where the mine shaft was, but all traces of the cottage are gone now and our father used the stone for hedging.

Until the middle of the 19th century, the South Tamar Mine below Weir Quay, had been worked northward, but when extremely rich lodes of silver lead were discovered, the mine was extended southward about 600 yards beneath the River Tamar. A smaller mine, known as the East Tamar Mine

Haye Farmhouse c.1999.

was also sunk and the mineshaft on Haye mash was part of that mine. It is said that hundreds of men were employed in these two mines in various capacities. However, in August 1856, one level, deep beneath the river, collapsed, flooding the whole of the South Tamar Mine, but fortunately the disaster occurred on a Sunday evening, when no men were underground. Attempts were made to try and seal the breach, as many thousands of pounds worth of ore was still unmined. This was around the time that Isambard Kingdom Brunel was at Saltash, supervising the building of the Royal Albert Rail Bridge and he was called in to give advice. But it was soon evident that the damage could not be rectified and the mine had to be abandoned. The collapse of the South Tamar Mine also affected the adjoining East Tamar Mine and that, too, was flooded and suffered a similar fate.

Local people have passed on this story over the years, but I believe it is true and there definitely was an unfenced mineshaft on Haye mash until the Water Authority made it safe in recent years. I believe the mine Captain's house was still occupied in the 1920s and the Cook family lived there at one time and after them came the Stainers. The last family to live there were friends of the Bridgemans.

When we lived at Haye Farm, it was just over one hundred acres, but it is bigger now, as fields which once belonged with Fursdon Farm and Strip Haye, are now part of Haye. At the present time, 1999, the farmhouse is unoccupied and Nigel Hunn rents the fields, but the Trust is renovating the property and it will probably be let again soon.

After Marjorie and Dorothy married and moved away, Kitty and I continued to live and work on the farm with our parents. During the Second World War a Prisoner of War camp was established at Callington. German and Italian prisoners were brought to various farms to work on the land and Father employed some at Haye. When the war ended and they were repatriated, the camp was used as a Hostel for those who had been granted political asylum. One of those Polish soldiers was sent to work on our farm. His name was Jozef Kusiak. Jozef told us his family were peasant farmers in Poland and when the country fell into Russian hands, German soldiers came to his home and captured him. He was twenty-one years old. At least one son from each family was taken prisoner. They were sent to Austria and Jozef worked for the Germans in a labour camp for three years. When the war ended he was freed, but Poland was still a communist country, so he went to Italy for a year or two in the Polish Free Army. He considered the possibility of seeking political asylum in Canada, but finally made his way to England, where he was granted leave to stay.

In 1952 Jozef and I married and we have two daughters, Josephine and Aniela (Nell). Jozef is eighty now and he has never once returned to his homeland. Josephine lives at Stone Cross with Ivan Cradick and they are just about to give up their market garden business. Nell has three children and she lives at Bohetherick, in the cottage that in the past was the village shop and known as Em's shop.

Jozef and I were living at Haye when our children were born, but in 1955 we went to live at Woodlands, where a century before my mother's forebears, the Vospers, had lived. In Sam Vosper's time, workers walked from Calstock to pick fruit at Woodlands. Then, the whole area was planted to strawberries, raspberries and fruit trees and dozens of people worked there on a casual basis. They used to stay all week in the packing shed, which at one period was used as a small jam-making store, and only return to their homes on Saturday night. On an old barn door, it was still possible to decipher a list of names, which had been written by the workers.

The place was very neglected when we went to live there and the land was in a poor state. We worked very hard to make a living for our family. We did all the work ourselves and did not employ anyone; it was not an easy time for us. Jozef and I gave up Woodlands in 1988 and retired to a cottage at Stone Cross.

Jim left Stockwell and farmed Haye when my father retired. I recall that Jim discovered a Second World War bomb embedded in the old dung pit at Stockwell when he was clearing up prior to moving to Haye.

Father spent the rest of his life at Newhouses where he was born. Generations of Maunders had lived in this particular house and records show that Maunders were residing there in 1843.

My grandfather Maunder was a woodsman on the Cotehele Estate and he was accidentally killed whilst felling a tree near Morden Hill.

At the turn of the century the Earl printed an address to his tenants in booklet form. It listed the names of the entire Estate workforce at that period and six Maunders were on that list. In later years, my father's sisters worked for Mr Langsford at the punnet factory at Cotehele Mill.

My great-grandfather on my mother's side was a miller at Radland Valley. Mother took me there once and showed me the remains of a wall which, she said formed part of the house where the Langsford's lived in the mid-1850s. Its difficult to prove what was there so many years ago; we just have to rely on what our parents told us and I think the original house was demolished years ago. It all belonged to the Snell family in the early days; the Langsfords were quite poor then and used to deliver sacks of grain astride the back of a donkey. There were so many in my mother's family, it's impossible to mention them all, but we do have a lovely photograph of Morden Farmhouse. I believe Mabel Langsford and then Horatio and Jane Langsford were tenants there in the past.

Morden Farm, once the home of George and Alice Langsford and their children Gerald, William and Zena. Note the 'Pole' barn.

We have the tenancy agreement between the Right Honourable Piers Alexander Hamilton, Earl of Mount Edgcumbe, and my Uncle George and Aunt Alice Langsford. It is dated 22 February 1938 and the rent for the fifty-one and a half-acre holding was £78 per annum. Attached, is the new agreement between the tenants and the new estate owners, The National Trust, dated 11 February 1954, when the rent was then raised to £108 per annum. Three acres were situated in the Parish of Calstock as they were across the millstream, which forms the parish boundary, the remainder of the land and the house being in St Dominick Parish.

Prior to them living at Morden, George Langsford had spent five years in America. Their daughter Zena was about five years old when Uncle George decided to go to Colorado to look for work in the gold mines. Aunt Alice and Zena followed at a later date and Zena's brothers, Gerald and William were born out there. On his return Uncle George had a coal business at Cotehele Quay and also worked Morden Farm.

A while back, some relations visited Colorado on holiday and they sent Zena a postcard depicting the street where Uncle George and his family had lived, showing the disused gold mines in the background. It is now a tourist area and no longer a mining town, but Zena said it was virtually unchanged and found it very interesting.

Zena was my cousin, but we were always very close and she used to telephone me everyday, but one day in December 1997 I didn't receive my usual call. My daughter Jo, went down to Newhouses and found that Zena had died whilst seated at the table having her breakfast. Everywhere was neat and tidy as usual and she had just passed quietly away at the age of 89.

I miss her very much and she was one of the few remaining members to bear the Langsford name.

Billiard team at Victory Hall. c.1940s.

Harold Maunder, Ernest Reep, Francis Hunn, Frank Steer, Alwyne Rickard, Les Nattle.

Back row: Miss Heath, Ken Rickard, Harry Martin, Fred Roberts, Fred Collins, Clifford Striplin, Ethel Medlin. *Middle row:* Ethel Cloake, Marion Herring, Geoffrey Mason, Marie Martin, Jean Martin, Inez Olver, Lorna Rickard, Donald Striplin, Wendell Fry, George Brown. *Front row:* Stuart Martin, Alwyne Rickard, Ernestine Herring, Marion Fry, Chrissie Hill, Phyllis Rickard, Doris Collins, Peter Sleep, Francis Wadge, Betty Rickard. *Kneeling:* Vivian Rogers, Jack Striplin. c.1930s.

CHAPTER NINE

As I strolled down Vogus Lane one windy autumn day, I was somewhat surprised to see a St Piran's flag fluttering from a make shift flag staff. At that point I realised I had discovered the village's most patriotic resident, so I decided to pay him a visit and ask if he was willing to have a chat with me about old times. The cottage door was opened by a bearded gentleman, who, had he been wearing a Cornish tartan kilt instead of the more conventional pair of trousers, could well have passed for one of Trelawney's men. This was my first meeting with Derrick Cradick.

"You did that 'Stitch in Time' book, didn't you?" he asked.

Apparently, that was a good enough recommendation and I was ushered indoors to meet his wife, Ernestine. This was the first time I had ever spoken to Mr and Mrs Cradick, but I was made very welcome.

I soon discovered that not only did Derrick fly the Cornish flag with pride, but was capable of conversing in his mother tongue too.

"What would you say if I said to you, 'Da dydh fatla genes?" quoted Derrick.

Wisely, noticing the wicked twinkle in his eye, I quickly replied, "I'd say no thankyou!" But I need not have worried. Apparently it was just a Cornish greeting and I should have replied, "Happy I am", or words to that effect. I never was any good at languages at school. But happy I was. Happy to listen to Derrick and his wife as they recalled some of the happenings in their sixty years of marriage, and the story of their close knit family.

I am also indebted to their daughter, Janet and her partner Alistair Tinto who invited me to their home, Lower Berry Cottage and devoted an entire Sunday afternoon to administering to my needs. It was so interesting to be actually sitting in the cottage that was mentioned so much by Joe Snell in his diaries, as Lower Berry Cottage was once the childhood home of his best mate Arnold Jope.

Alistair, knowing of my growing interest in my ancestors, had already prepared pages of information pertaining to the Langsfords of St Dominick, which I was delighted to obtain. I only had to mention some query about a name or a date and Alistair's computer was thrown into top gear and the printed results made available to me in a few seconds.

Who would ever have expected to find a branch of the Cornwall Records Office hidden away in the middle of Radland Wood!

Janet also phoned various members of her family in an attempt to obtain dates and other snippets of information I required and this was a tremendous help.

I am grateful for the willing support given me by Alistair and Janet and other members of the Cradick family. The results of their joint efforts are now included in Derrick and Ernestine's story.

Man of Kernow

by Derrick Cradick

Derrick Cradick in the Home Guard. c.1940s.

I am Derrick Cradick, one of four sons born to Leonard and Edith Cradick *née* Maunder. I was born in 1915 in the cottage next door to where John Friendship now lives, in Baber Lane. My brothers were Alec, Douglas and Gordon.

When my father was a young man he spent some years in Australia and the USA. He worked as a miner; a farmer and he helped to lay gas pipes during the time when gas was becoming more widespread in the United States.

For many years my dad worked a three and a half-acre field at Stockwell Farm, where my mum's brother Harold Maunder lived at that time. Dad grew cherries, Bramley and Jubilee apples and soft fruit of every description.

Derrick, Alec, Douglas and Gordon Cradick. *c*.1939.

I attended St Dominick Church School and when I was fourteen we moved to Greenbank Farm, on the banks of the River Tamar near Halton Quay. Dad rented about twenty acres from the Pentillie Estate, we kept a few cows and pigs, but it was mainly a market garden, with a few cherry trees too.

In 1938, Dad bought a cottage at Glebe in Vogus Lane. He bought it from Arthur Martin for £260. Postman Jack Hooper had once lived there and he was also a saddler by trade. The workshop still stands in the garden and the cottage is now known as Saddlers Cottage.

In 1938 I married Ernestine Herring, who lived at Bohetherick Farm with her parents Freeman and Mabel and her sister Marion. The farm was Edgcumbe property and now belongs to the National Trust. Ernestine's sister, Marion, married Fred Rogers' youngest son, Vivian.

We lived in Saddlers Cottage when we married and stayed until 1956. That was when Ernestine's father died. Her mother moved to Tor View and we took over the tenancy of Bohetherick Farm, where we lived with our four children, Tony, Ivan, Julian and Janet.

Lucy Jope *née* Trease, wife of William Jope, Smeaton Farm and Eliza Herring *née* Bowden wife of Edmund (Ned) Herring, Bohetherick Farm taken at St Dominick Rectory. *c*.1940.

Until Freeman Herring's death, I had been working at Greenbank most of the time with my dad and brother Douglas. But Dad died in 1955, when he was 68 and soon after Dad's death mum left Greenbank and moved to the now vacant Saddlers Cottage and remained there until her death in 1977 aged 86. Douglas stayed on the farm until 1958, he then moved into Callington and became a Postman. He has one son Keith. When the Cradicks finally left Greenbank, Mr and Mrs John Bailek went there. They retired in 1994 and now live in a retirement bungalow at Cross.

All of us boys worked on the land most of our lives. When my brother Alec married Marie Martin, they went to live at Jubilee Cottages and worked six acres at Halton Wood. Albert Reep rented the adjoining few acres and he lived at Hill Brow. Alec has one daughter, Susan, who lives in the village, but sadly Alec's wife died recently.

Jack Talbot took on Alec's land when he retired, but it is not being worked now and his packing house by Halton Road has been demolished.

My brother Gordon died in 1971, but he and his wife Marion had lived and worked at Strawberry Hill alongside Albert Wills. They lost their only daughter Sharon when she was in her early thirties.

In the 1960s while we were at Bohetherick Farm, we took over Ernest and Lewis Reep's orchard. We grew a lot of cherries there and we had to use forty bar ladders to reach the tops of the tallest trees. More recently, as the old trees began to die out, the Trust decided to replant the orchards with young cherry trees. These were grafted by James Evans and Mick Downing helped to plant them when he worked for the Trust. I believe the young trees are growing well but it takes years before they produce a decent crop of fruit.

We retired in 1977, when I was 62 and our son Tony took over the tenancy of Bohetherick Farm and he still lives there. It is quite a large farm with land reaching down to the riverbank alongside Woodlands. Our other son, Ivan has worked a market garden down there for many years. He is about to give up that land and just concentrate on the large garden which surrounds his home at Stone Cross. Ivan's first marriage broke up in 1977, so when we left the farm Ernestine and I moved into Ivan's house and helped him out for three years. While we were there we had Saddlers Cottage

Friends and family, on the occasion of Marion and Gordon Cradick's wedding.

Threshing day at Bohetherick
Farm. The 'pole' barn still
exists. c.1930s.

renovated and that is where we have lived since 1980. We are now back in the same house where we started our married life over sixty years ago. I rent a field opposite our cottage; it is Glebe land and is useful to store wood and to park a car when our family visits us. We are very lucky to have all our children living so near, especially as Ernestine cannot get about so well lately.

Our son, Julian and his wife Yvonne have recently bought the mill house at Radland. Julian has two daughters from a previous marriage and he and Yvonne have twin girls and they love living there. By today's standards it is isolated, but ideal for the children. The mill house is the only habitable building left in the hamlet now, and Joe Snell once worked the ground as a market garden. It has not been cultivated for over thirty years. Joe Snell was a good boxer; he would take on anybody in the boxing booths at Honey Fair or Goose Fair at Tavistock and went to watch any famous boxers who came to Plymouth for a match. He taught the Taylor boys and the Bennetts to box when they all lived down Radland Mill in the 1920s and 30s. I took up boxing a bit when I was trying to get fit after a serious illness when I was nineteen. I spent months in hospital at St Agnes being cared for by Nuns. My parents didn't approve of me boxing, they thought I should take gentle exercise to build up my strength, not do something as dangerous as boxing. But I did it just the same without their knowledge. I boxed under the name of Jack Smith and had bouts in the Public Hall in Liskeard and in Callington and didn't come to any harm.

In later years I developed farmer's lung and was no longer able to work on the farm. John and Herbert Davy in Saltash gave me a job delivering meat. I also worked as a driver at Treburley abattoir.

Our daughter, Janet has inherited her grandfather's wanderlust, she and her first husband travelled widely for many years. Janet now lives with her partner Alistair Tinto, at Lower Berry, in Radland Woods. We bought the property from the Jope family in the 1970s. It used to be a pair of cottages and Evelyn and Wilfred Kitt and Aubrey Gale and his wife, were the last tenants. Janet has converted it into one home now. She has two sons, Reuben is a student at the Duchy Farm College at Stoke Climsland and he is very interested in farming. Jamie goes to Devonport High School with his cousin Howard who is about the same age, they are great mates. They both passed the entrance exam when they were pupils at St Dominick School.

At the start of the Second World War, all the chaps who were exempt from joining the Forces because they were doing essential work on the land, were expected to join the Home Guard. Some of us keen ones volunteered right away, but it soon became compulsory for all men under sixty to enlist, unless medically unfit. In the beginning we were known as the Local Defence Volunteers, but it was later changed to the Home Guard. Butcher Martin's son Arthur, had been a soldier in the First World War and when the Home Guard was formed in St Dominick, he was made Lieutenant of the

Ida Bridgeman, Betty Hocking and Mabel Herring.

Platoon. Owen Rogers from up Churchtown and Leonard Hughes from Danescombe were Sergeants and we met in the Victory Hall every Sunday morning for lectures and training. We went to Tregantle Fort to practice our shooting skills on the rifle range. Half a dozen of us were on duty each night patrolling the lanes round about. I was sent to London on an Officer's Course and I learnt signalling, map reading, the lot. I really took to it and became one of the youngest officers around the district. As such, I was chosen to meet King George VI. when he visited Canon Andrews, our Colonel-in Chief, at Stoke Climsland. I had a really good time in the Home Guard and by the time the war was over we were ready for anything!

I've always been interested in the Cornish language. I attended evening classes at Liskeard for a while. I can speak a little Cornish and I seem to recall that someone from the Old Cornwall Society, came to St Dominick school in Miss Moon's time and taught us a bit of Cornish, but French is considered more important now, because we are in the European Market. I have some Cornish language tapes, which Janet gave me and I try to learn a bit from them. I fly my St Piran's flag in my field across the road. I am proud of being a 'Man of Kernow'.

Butcher Jim Reep of Baber House. c.1950s.

W. Rosekilly. Farmer at Lower Baber Farm. c.1930s.

The Earl and Countess Mount Edgcumbe opening a church fete. Janet Cradick is second child from left. The man on the right is Lawrence Maker (Callington). Also in the picture the Reverend Ralph and Addice Perry-Gore. Reverend Perry-Gore was Rector at St Dominick 1946–1959. Ten years later they retired to Tortola, an island they owned in the Caribbean. He lived there for the rest of his life, his wife having pre-deceased him whilst on a return visit to Cornwall, c. early 1950s.

Butcher Reep's three daughters, Freda, Edna and Amy taught elocution and music in the village.

CHAPTER TEN

Vera Duke was one of the first people to respond to my appeal for information and photographs for inclusion in this book and how glad I am she took the trouble to contact me.

When I visited her she spoke fluently of her memories of the past 50 years. To my delight she produced a letter and photograph pertaining to the period when Italian and German prisoners of war were brought to the village from Callington to work on the land during the war. She was happy to allow me to publish this very touching letter. Then she offered me a photograph depicting her mother-in-law's ancestors. I was amazed to see that this photograph was taken outside Tipwell Cottage – the very house my own mother was born in on 20th November 1897. I am so pleased to be able to print this photograph which is of such interest to my sister and I.

As I left Vera's home, I met her neighbour Max O'Dowd who was busily mowing his lawn. Whilst working for the Co-op, Max delivered milk around the Parish in all weathers for 28 years. I mentioned that I hoped to publish another book shortly and Max replied "I don't think you should publish all the things I got up to when I was a milkman, but you can mention that you came across an 'Old Codger' pushing the last remaining cylinder mower left in the Parish!" joked Max. I must admit it was the most ancient piece of machinery I had come across in my travels!

The Duke Family

by Vera Duke

Raymond and Vera Duke on their wedding day. c.1948.

My family link with the village goes back as far as the First World War, when my Aunt Nell Smith met up with a St Dominick man, Ernest Cradick when he was billeted in Northampton.

They married and came back here to live after the war. Aunt Nell's brother Jack used to work in a shoe factory in the Midlands but he developed chest problems and was advised to give up his factory work and get an outdoor job. When he was seventeen, Jack Smith came to St Dominick to join his sister and he got a job working for Mr Reginald Langsford at Birchenhayes Farm and he 'lived-in' there for some years and worked mainly in the market garden until his marriage to Nora Babb in 1933. They have two children, Ralph and Brenda. Although he is now in his 89th year and has spent so long in St Dominick, he has never lost his Midland's accent.

Uncle Ernest and Aunt Nell moved to Kelly Bray and Uncle drove for the Co-op bakery and later for butcher Rundle at Callington. During the Second World War, my mother and little sister lived down here with Aunt Nell for some time and I stayed in London with Dad. However, when the flying bombs struck London, Dad said I must move down here for safety too. I was

Edward Rickard, his daughter Emily Maunder grandson Charlie Maunder and granddaughter Lily Maunder (later Duke) outside Tipwell House. Edward was Raymond Duke's great-grandfather. c.1900.

seventeen when I arrived to stay with Uncle Jack and his wife in 1944 and I never returned to London. I worked on the land with Uncle Jack as by this time they were living in a farmhouse at Burraton and had a market garden.

Before the Council houses were built at Cross it was the meeting place for a whole crowd of teenagers. On Sunday evening Valerie and Raymond Duke, Lewis Rickard, Joan Williams, Joyce Rickard, Alwyne Rickard, Courtney Vanstone, Doreen and David Rickard, Nesta Babb, Wyn Sambles, Betty Rogers, Gordon Cradick, Geoff Martin and I would get together and amble up Smeaton Hill and out to Vernigo crossroads. It was all very innocent and we never caused any trouble, we just amused ourselves and chatted. We were all saddened when Lewis Rickard died quite suddenly in his early twenties. He lived down Vogus Lane and was a lovely lad and well-liked.

Many of that generation married quite young, the girls being about eighteen years old. Raymond Duke and I went out together and we married at St Dominick Church in 1948 and we held our reception in the schoolroom. For the first five years after our marriage we lived in rooms at Uncle Jack's house and our eldest son Mervyn was born during that time. Mervyn is keen on tractor work and he works for Nigel Hunn. Our other son, Christopher, lives in the Garden Cottage at Pentillie Castle and does gardening and maintenance work for Mrs Coryton. He trained as a butcher, but prefers outdoor work and is very happy where he is at present.

Jack and Lily Duke on their wedding day.
Jack died in 1961 aged 62.
Lily died in 1992 aged 101.

Oswald Lorenz, a German prisoner of war, who worked for Jack and Lily Duke. c.1946.

When the Council houses were built here at Cross, Raymond and I rented one and I have lived here now for forty-six years. My husband worked on the land all his life. His parents John (Jack) and Lily Duke *née* Maunder took ground at Burcombe Wood in 1933 and when Raymond left school he worked with them. George Finch had land alongside and when we married we took over his adjoining land and worked that as well. The entrance to our market garden was down a lane opposite the entrance to Chapel Farm on the Halton Quay road. We had to go through Dairy Mill farmyard to reach our ground. The land was rented from the Pentillie Estate, but after Major Coryton's death it was sold off. It is now incorporated in Peter Batten's farm at Burcombe and is no longer a market garden. There were a lot of American Mother apple trees on the land and we also grew cherries, beans, strawberries, daffodils, anemones and cabbage and Raymond kept pigs down there in a meadow.

Raymond and Valerie's Dad died in 1961, but his mother was a very lively person and she carried on helping us until Raymond gave up the ground in 1965. Raymond worked for Peter Batten then and later for Tom Gorman at Fursdon and at Nigel Hunns after that. Sadly in 1991 after a short illness Raymond died, he was only 63 years old.

I worked at various jobs until I was 65. When we married I always helped on our market garden and when we gave that up I took a job in the restaurant of the 'Who'd have Thought It' Inn and later in Gatsbury's which was a café in Callington and I was nurse maid to Mr and Mrs Grenfell's little girl, Suzanne, from when she was three months old till she was two. I used to go to their bungalow up Tipwell road next door

4-3-46
CAMP CALLINGTON
CORNWALL

DEAR BOSS

I AM JUST WRITING THIS LETTER TO LET you KNOW THAT I AM GOING MY HOME NEXT WEEK, I SHALL BE VERY HAPPY,

FOR THAT I DO NOT KNOW HOW I THANKS ever so MUCH FOR YOUR HOSPITALITY AND KINDNESS THAT you HAVE HAD ABOUT ME WHEN I WORKED YOUR FARM AS you were POLITE WITH ME,

WELL DEAR BOS I AM TELLING TO YOU IF I HAVE CHANCE IN WEEK TIME I SHOULD LIKE TO COME YOUR HOME TO SEE YOU AGAIN BEFORE I TO GO MY HOME I HOPE eys,

AND NOW MYSELF SEND YOU TOGETHE ALL REST YOUR FAMILY ALL MY BEST WISHING AND SO I WISH TO YOU AND YOUR NICE FAMILY ALL BEST FOR ever, SO I WILL CLOSE NOW TO SAY TO YO AND YOUR FAMILY (GOOD-BYE FOR ever) MAY GOD ALWAYS BLESS you FROM YOUR FAITHFUL An

Italian Prisoner of War, Angelo, who wrote such a touching letter of thanks to Lily and Jack, prior to his return to Italy after the Second World War. c.1946.

to Gaythorne. I also looked after Diana Iron's two little children. Diana used to bring Alexandra and Athwenna here and I looked after them in my own home.

Jack and Lily Duke first lived at Bohetherick but moved to the new Council houses at Trehill Cross when they were completed in 1939. Their neighbours were Mr and Mrs Cyril Striplin and their sons Alfie and Donald. Lily worked hard all her life. When during the war they had German and Italian prisoners of war helping on the land, she used to cook up good meals for them which they appreciated very much. The prisoners, who were billeted in a camp at Moss Side where Ginsters pasty factory is now, used to come to work with just a hunk of bread and cheese to last them all day. Raymond's mother used to say "You can't expect them to do a good day's work without proper food inside them". She was very good to them. One German and an Italian kept in contact when they returned to their own countries and wrote very kind letters to thank 'Boss and his wife' for their kindness. I still have those letters and their photographs, but they are both dead now.

After we gave up the ground at Burcombe Wood, Raymond's mother spent a lot of time working in the greenhouses at Little Smeaton, helping her niece, Phyllis Morrish to prick out seedlings and bunch flowers for market.

She carried on working until failing eyesight prevented her doing the job and she lived to a great age, proving that hard work never hurt any body!

She died in 1992 aged 101.

CHAPTER ELEVEN

Another branch of local history I hoped to record was that of the life and work of Richard Striplin and his son Stanley. So my next visit was to the home of Sylvia Mason, Stan's only daughter.

I personally, do not remember Mr Striplin senior, but I do remember visiting Stan at his carpenter's shop in Baber Lane. As a child I use to accompany my dad when he went to collect replacement bars for our ladders, prior to the fruit-picking season and occasionally Stan was asked by my father to make a new ladder for him. This did not happen very often as the timber used in ladder making in those days was of such good quality that, combined with the craftsmanship of the local carpenter, the ladders lasted from one generation to another.

I was also a regular visitor to the village shop each Saturday and here I remember being served by Stan Striplin's daughter Sylvia. We bought the 'Cornish Times', 'Christian Herald' and 'Farmer & Stock Breeder' from 'shop' and usually the weekly budget stretched to a quarter pound of Nuttal's Mintoes, which were weighed on the brass scales and carefully put into a little cone shaped paper bag. Occasionally, we bought a Lyons Madeira cake which, in the period I remember, was sold in a red, white and blue cardboard carton. Isn't it strange how such small details remain in ones memory for so many years?

When I called on Sylvia at her home in the village, I was only expecting to learn something about the lives of her father and grandfather. To my surprise I was also given an insight into her husband Geoffrey's young life, as he told me that despite working on his father's market garden at Little Braunder during the war, he was called up for war service.

This piece of information was an added bonus as I had interviewed the Mason family in my previous book 'A Stitch in Time' and no one had mentioned this period in Geoffrey's life. Apparently as their acreage was small and the fact his elder brother Cecil and his sister Hilda also worked in the family business the 'powers that be' decreed that Geoffrey could not be exempted, so the youngest member of the family joined the Army.

Geoffrey remembers that Reg Barker from Jubilee Cottages; also left the village on the same day and he joined the Royal Navy.

Consequently Geoffrey Mason was abroad on active service for three years. He proudly showed me a scrapbook he prepared after his return, which gives a very clear indication of his time in the Royal Signal Corps. Photographs of himself and comrades enjoying their free periods visiting places of interest, even menu's from cafes they frequented, were all neatly displayed, along with his de-mob papers and cap badge. In a box, especially made for the purpose by his grandson whilst still at school, were Geoffrey's ribbons and medals carefully wrapped in a chamois cloth and resting on the velvet lining. An interesting and sentimental momento of the Second World War, to pass on to future generations.

I am delighted to include a mention of Geoffrey's war service alongside his wife's memories of a much loved grandfather and her parents – the Striplin family

The Striplin Story

by Sylvia Mason

I am Sylvia Mason *née* Striplin and I live with my husband Geoffrey at 1 Baber Cottage opposite the Ebenezer Chapel at St Dominick.

My grandparents were Richard and Mary Louise Striplin (*née* Doidge). They had four children, William Doidge Striplin, Bertha Louisa, Lily Helena and Stanley John.

William went to the U.S.A. at an early age, came home for some years then returned there for the rest of his life.

Bertha married the village carpenter Cecil Jane, and they had one son Donald George and a daughter, Lily Louisa. She was two weeks younger then me, but little Lily died of appendicitis when she was only seven years old.

Richard and Mary Louisa Striplin. c.1914.

Aunt Lily was a cripple and remained a spinster and lived with her parents in their cottage in Baber Lane. In 1889, eleven months after Lily's birth, Stanley was born and he was my father. Grandfather Richard was a wheelwright and carpenter and his two sons learned their trade from him, as did Cecil Jane.

When Stanley was a teenager he too, went to the U.S.A., where he joined his brother. He was only permitted to enter America because he had a job awaiting him with his brother in a carpenter's shop. The two worked together servicing the copper mines until the First World War broke out. Stan had become an American citizen and he joined the American Field Artillery and served in France and Germany until the end of the war. He returned to the U.S.A. on 11th June 1919 and at the end of that year he returned to the United Kingdom.

He married Ada Rickard in 1920 and in 1923 I was born. I was their only child. My parent's first home was at Kelly Park.

I never knew my grandmother as she died on 19th May when I was six weeks old. My grandfather was known as 'Dicky Box' because he was the village undertaker and made all the coffins. He was a wonderful carpenter and I have a pitch pine, glass fronted buffet and also a corner cupboard, which he made. When Stan married, his father made the couple a cupboard, which I have also inherited. Both my father and my grandfather made carts and wagons for the local farmers and also the long ladders used by the fruit pickers in the cherry and apple orchards, which surrounded the village in those days. I have a photograph, which shows grandfather making his last cherry ladder when he was 86 years old.

Richard Striplin helped to rip ground that later became known as Brentswood. Mr James Langsford and his father-in-law Mr Parken, ripped the first six acres nearest Birchenhayes Farm and Richard took over the next couple of acres. All the woodland trees that grew there at that period in the 1880s, were blasted out with dynamite and the ground dug by men using viskeys. Richard

Striplin planted up the area with fruit trees and strawberry plants. He also built a wooden stable for his horse and a two-storey shed on the lower side of the path, where he prepared his daily food and stored and packed his produce. As time went by and other men of his generation took on similar tasks, soon the whole valley was cultivated. Grandfather built some of the packing sheds in other parts of Brentswood and also one at nearby Crocadon Wood near St Mellion. A large area of ground on the slopes of Crocadon Wood was ripped by Stan Striplin when he returned from America and I can remember travelling there with my father in his pony and trap. I recall seeing Mrs Laura Langsford holding her little toddler, Pamela, in her arms as we went by as we had to pass Birchenhayes farmhouse to reach both my father's and my grandfather's market gardens. That must have been around 1929. The ground at Crocadon soon went back to scrub land after my father gave it up in the mid-1930s. Ten years later this ground was again brought back into production, when Sid Barker from Jubilee Cottages, took over the land and worked it for a number of years. It is woodland again now, but I have been told that the packing house that my grandfather built was still there up until a few years ago. Geoffrey never visited my family's ground at Brentswood, but he remembers that Richard Striplin and Cecil Jane came to Braunder at Halton Quay and built a garage to house his father, Nelson's first car.

Richard was remarkable in that he always carried all his measurements in his head, and was never known to write anything down. He could estimate the amount of timber required for a job and when it was completed there would only be a couple of inches of timber over. On the occasion when he was building Nelson Mason's garage he came home and said, "When I got down there, that young boy had been at me tools again". That was Geoffrey! He had been trying out the different tools and playing about with them. That garage still exists.

Grandfather used to go down to Plymouth docks in Jack Taylor's haulage lorry and there he would pick the exact pieces of timber he wanted for a job, also the spars for ladders. They had to be perfect, especially when he was making cherry ladders. He bought oak for the bars and they had to be free of knots or they would break in use. Everything was handmade and shaping the bars was called 'nogging'. If on occasion Jack's lorry was loaded by someone else, Grandfather would examine the timber when it was delivered and if it was not the actual pieces he had originally chosen he would not except it and it would be returned to the timber yard.

Grandfather kept three cows and they sold raw and scalded milk and cream to the villagers. Aunt Lily also made butter for sale.

When Grandfather got too old to do so much work, my father gave up market gardening and worked in the carpenter shop behind their cottage full time and helped with the undertaker's business until Grandfather's death. Grandfather died on the 31st January 1940 aged 89.

My father continued the business until his health failed. He always enjoyed visiting butcher Jim Reep at Baber House. They would talk together in the evenings whilst Edna was giving her music lessons. He also spent a lot of time with Fred Rickard who lived in what was once Polly Bennett's sweet shop. Mr and Mrs Rawlings live there now.

After my mother died in 1961, father continued to live in the cottage with his sister Aunt Lily. But he eventually went into St Mary's Home at Launceston and he died there on the 30th December 1977, when he was 88 years old.

Aunt Lily stayed on at the cottage alone for a while after her brother went to St Mary's, but she had a bad fall and was very ill. She did not want to go into hospital, so Geoffrey took two weeks holiday, he was working for Alan Rickard up at Lanoyce Nurseries at the time, and we stayed with Aunt Lily night and day for a fortnight. This was during the time that Reverend Rendall was Rector here and he spent a lot of time at the cottage with us and was very kind. Lily died in 1974 at the age of 86, in the home where she had spent her entire life.

Geoffrey worked for Alan Rickard, Westlake's eldest son, for some time after the Mason family gave up Little Braunder in 1971 and he eventually retired in 1988. Geoffrey served in the Second World War. He joined the Army on the 7th January 1943 and saw service in Algiers, Tunis, Sicily, Italy, and Corsica, the South of France, Norway and Greece. He was in the Royal Corps of Signals.

He brought home various souvenirs from his trips to foreign parts and he made a scrapbook that gives details of the exact dates he sailed between each country and photographs of interest. His wage was two shillings (10p) a day when he joined the Army, but had risen to three shillings by the time he was demobbed in July 1946. Among the items in his scrapbook is the invitation to attend a 'Welcome Home' celebration at the church schoolroom after the war. Fred Rogers, on behalf of the Welcome Home Committee signed the invitation. Each returning serviceman was presented with a cheque for £25.

My cousin, Donald Jane also served in the Second World War, his teenage years were spent working at Birchenhayes Farm, but he joined the Royal Navy soon after the outbreak of war and was away from the area for many years. When he was young his best friend was Raymond Martin, who at that time worked for Arthur Martin at Bohetherick. Raymond's family lived near Donald in a cottage that was later demolished. Little Coombe House has since been built on the site. They use to attend church together and were bellringers. Raymond died about a year ago, but Donald and his wife Constance live in Callington and we see them frequently. He is 80 years old.

Richard Striplin aged 86 making his last cherry ladder. c.1938.

After I left school I trained as a hairdresser. I did a three-year apprenticeship with Mrs Squance at Callington. But during the war years I worked part-time on the Telephone Exchange at St Dominick Post Office, a job that I enjoyed very much. The remainder of the time I worked on the land for Mr Fred Hancock at Baber Farm. I also went potato picking at Eastcott with Amy Reep. I helped out at the village shop and Post Office for a number of years in Ethel Ford's time and other girls who worked there in those days, were Daisy Gorman, who's brother Bill took over Tipwell Farm and Kathleen Rosekilly, whose father farmed Lower Baber (now a housing estate). Kathleen married Donald Borlace and they had two children Sonia and Kevin.

Geoffrey and I married in 1947 and we have lived in this house for 52 years. We have one daughter Sandra and she is married to Trevor Annear, who is the deputy head-teacher at Saltash Comprehensive School. He travels to work from his home in Bodmin every day. Sandra has worked for Bricknell's Store in the town for a number of years. We have two grandchildren now in their early twenties. Charles works as a computer analyst at Bournemouth University and our granddaughter Kathryn works for the Department of the Environment at Bodmin.

Youngsters today have a very different lifestyle from ours and we have seen a lot of changes in the village in our lifetime.

CHAPTER TWELVE

As soon as I arrived for my evening appointment with Gerald and Joyce Veale in their lovely home overlooking a wide sweep of the River Tamar near Cotehele, I was greeted warmly. I knew they were happy to help me with my project as their photo album was already on the table awaiting my perusal! Having spent most of my school days with Gerald's sister Loveday, I felt a little more confident in their company than I had with some other villagers I had interviewed. In this case I was familiar with the family names that were bandied about in the course of our conversation.

I well remember Gerald's parents and their bungalow at Oak Tree as I had often visited Loveday there when we were teenagers. Their adopted daughter Joyce was a friend of my sister, which reminds me of an incident that we often laugh about although it happened many years ago. My sister Pamela, Joyce and I were attending a service at the Trinity Chapel and small collection envelopes had been set out on the pews for the congregation to donate cash for some foreign mission. All was well until, during a rather boring sermon Joyce spied a large spider scurrying over our hymn books in front of us. She quickly opened the flap of her envelope and the poor unsuspecting creature crawled inside and was promptly sealed in much to our amusement! Not a very charitable thing to do, but to our young minds it was hilarious and we had to spend the rest of the service trying to stifle our giggles. Isn't it strange how childhood pranks always stay in your memory! But there were no tricks to be played tonight and no Joyce to share this memory with, as she went to Canada to live many years ago and she only makes the occasional visit back to St Dominick.

Even the Chapel where this incident occurred has not stood the test of time; Trinity Chapel was demolished in 1991 and a new house now stands on the site.

As we talked together other memories were revived outside the realms of market gardening which I was supposedly pursuing.

Gerald's wife Joyce was the daughter of Henry and Flossie Collins and Henry and his eldest son Fred used to run a threshing business in the district during the 1930s and 40s. Every year they came to my father's farm, Birchenhayes to do a days thresh. Fred related his story of his life with the steam engine and threshing machine in a chapter of my book 'A Stitch in Time'. He was the Fred Dibnah of Jan Dominick in the past and his tales were a welcome addition to my book.

During the war instead of going into the forces Joyce's sister Doris joined her father and brother and worked along-side the men on the threshing machine. Doris endured all the heat and the dust through the long threshing season and also helped her parents on their market garden at Stockwell during the summer months.

Joyce Collins outside her hairdressing salon, Fore Street Callington c.1949.

Joyce remembered that her mother had worked for my Aunt Alberta Martin at Towell Farm for years. She cleaned the dairy equipment scrubbed the vast slate kitchen floor and washed all Uncle Gilbert's dustcoats and overalls. Joyce and her younger brother Joe spent hundreds of hours at Towell playing in the fields and barns whilst their mother worked in the house. Joyce used to tease my Aunt Alberta by ringing her door bell and running away and Aunty would shout after her "You faggot it's you again!" We all had such a happy and innocent childhood in those days with none of the fears and temptations that face our children and grand-children today.

By the time Joyce left school the war was over and she decided to follow a more lady-like pursuit. She learnt her trade as a hairdresser and ran a business in Fore Street Callington for some years. I was one of her customers and I recall having my hair permed by her. In those days it was a rather hazardous event. My hair was trimmed, washed and dried, then rolled on to heavy metal curlers, doused with a variety of evil smelling chemicals and then attached to hot overhead wires, where I remained partially suspended for some hours. Or so it seemed to me, no doubt it was a much more technical procedure and was very skilfully performed. It was quite the norm to suffer a few burnt ear lobes despite the wads of cotton wool which were stuffed into every conceivable cavity between the hot curlers. After a few hours I emerged smelling slightly of singed hair, but with the compulsory rolls of little sausage-like curls surrounding my face, happy in the knowledge that Joyce had done her best once again, to try and make a silk purse out of a sow's ear!

All this suffering was deemed necessary at least once a year if one had any chance of capturing the attention of a partner at the local Saturday night dance!

At this period, the late 1940s I was working just across the street from Joyce's salon at the Market Stores, a double fronted shop that had previously been Alford's grocery store. My boss was George Seddon and although I worked alone in the fruit shop there were several other staff in the grocery department. Jim Taylor drove the big 'Dads Army' type delivery van that was used to take grocery orders to outlying villages and farms. Jim's wife Christine and Marie Deacon and her cousin Albert Jacketts worked behind the counter. Sadly Albert was killed in a motor bike accident whilst still a young man.

Certain basic commodities were still rationed when I worked at the Market Stores. Part of my job entailed counting the coupons which customers had to deposit with us in order to obtain their weekly ration of fats, cheese, sugar, tea and sweets. Sugar and the occasional issue of dried fruit was delivered to us in large sacks and these had to be weighed into 2oz, 4oz or 8oz portions and then be placed in strong paper bags and the tops folded over securely — no cellotape in those days! Butter and lard arrived in large blocks weighing several pounds and these had to be weighed meticulously to make sure that each customer received their exact entitlement. The Market Stores took over a bakery at Looe and my fruit shop then became a cake shop. One of the delivery drivers was Bernard Harding (now of Trebrownbridge), he was always full of fun and used to eat raw bacon off the counter as he said it made him passionate!

We were a happy crowd and I enjoyed my years at the shop. Joyce and I recalled the shops that have long since closed or been demolished. Biscombes, Dicken's Haberdashery, Trelevans who sold clothes and hats, Buckinghams the saddler, Jane's tailor shop, Langman's Bakery, Follys sweet shop, Coles, Oakes and Attwoods. What memories all these names invoked.

Joyce and I used to travel to Callington on the bus and I still have the last Weekly Return ticket I bought whilst working at the Market Stores. The fare was 2 shillings (10 pence) a week and I paid a shilling a day for my two course lunch at Chubbs Hotel. All the workers used to eat there. My wage started at £1.1.0d a week, but by the time I left I was earning the princely sum of £1.7.8d. Joyce reminded me that a perm would have cost me £2 then, so I think my parents must have subsidised that little luxury.

Joyce had a moment of fame in 1947 when she was chosen to be Callington's Carnival Queen. Her attendants were Margaret Moore and Beryl Owen. As well as presiding over the town's carnival parade that year Joyce attended a number of Carnivals around the district. This was of course the year of the Royal Wedding. In 1997 Callington decided to celebrate the Queen's Golden Wedding by inviting local couples who were celebrating their own Golden Weddings, to a reception in the Town Hall. Joyce having been the town's Carnival Queen in 1947 was invited to attend. She and Gerald were taken to the reception by taxi and it was a Right Royal Do!

Joyce still practises her hairdressing and over the years this has been very much appreciated by her older and housebound clients. It is very convenient for local people to have someone prepared to visit their homes if necessary, to trim or perm their hair. Perming techniques have changed completely over the past 50 years and the old equipment has long since become redundant along with the skills of the hairdressers of that era. Cold perms and plastic curlers are much less hazardous and therefore much simpler to use. Joyce sold her business three years after she married Gerald. Since then she has shared the work of Gerald's market garden, brought up two sons, continued with her hairdressing from her home and performed all the duties of running a household and ensuring that Gerald's fried breakfast appears promptly every morning!

"The fat in a good fried breakfast won't hurt you providing you get out and do a days hard work afterwards" Gerald assured me.

He certainly is proof of that as just a few months off his 75th birthday he looks at least ten years younger and is as slim and upright as he was 40 years ago!

"I have no intention of stopping work for years yet" said Gerald and as long as Gerald keeps going I'm sure Joyce will carry on in her supporting role.

"I've always loved bunching flowers, I love my hairdressing and the housework isn't a problem, though sometimes I'd like a bit of help indoors, but I'm happy as I am and I would do the same things over again" said Joyce with a smile.

After a refreshing cup of tea I decided it was time to get down to the real purpose of my visit, to hear how Gerald had spent 60 years as a market gardener in the Tamar Valley.

And this is Gerald's story.

The Veales of Clements House

by Gerald Veale

In the 1920s my father Ethelred and his twin brother Alfred lived in the two adjoining houses at Mount Pleasant and that is where I, Gerald Veale, was born on 2nd January 1925.

Father had eight other brothers, five of whom went to America or Canada in their youth. One brother Fernley lived in Ryelands Cottage at Vernigo, which our grandfather Johnny Veale built. He also had four sisters Polly, Gertrude, Blanche and Mable. My mother was Jane Rogers and she came from a big family too.

We lived in the cottage nearest St Dominick and when Uncle Alfred moved to Altarnun, our new neighbours were, Eber Johns and his family.

Around 1936 we left Mount Pleasant and went to live at Chaybel Farm (Chapel Farm) down near Halton Quay. We only stayed there two years, because our cattle kept dying of a disease that they caught when grazing the mash (marshes). Father heard there were two fields of about ten acres further up the valley, which were at that period being worked by Eric Martin and Fred Rogers. He decided to leave the farm and concentrate on market gardening. That is when the Veales took over this ground, Lodge Gardens. I was glad because I didn't like milking and knew, even at that early age that I did not want to be a farmer.

In 1938 Father had a bungalow built in a field up by Oak Tree and they named it Trenear. It cost £400 to build and two weeks after completion Fred Rogers offered Father £800 for it, but Father

Gerald Veale with his first car at Vernigo cross *c.*1942.

Joyce Veale and her mother Jane at 'Trenear' *c.*1947.

declined. My parents lived there for the rest of their lives and worked the ten acres until they retired in 1956.

From the time I left school at fourteen I had always worked for my father, so naturally I took over when he retired.

In 1951 I married Joyce Collins and we lived at the Lodge for 34 years renting it from the National Trust. Both our sons, Andrew and Peter were born there. At the time of our marriage Joyce had a hairdressing business in Callington and she worked there for a couple of years after our marriage. She has always kept on hairdressing in a small way, either working from home or visiting elderly people in their houses, fitting it in with flower bunching and the housework.

Fred Rickard, Joyce Veale, Ethelred Veale c.1953.

Soon after Father retired another three acres of ground owned privately by Lewis Reep was offered to me. I wasn't keen on taking it on, I thought we had enough to do with the original ten acres we rented from the National Trust, but Father persuaded me and my brother-in-law Mick Downing to go for it. It cost £400 per acre and would make five times that today so I am glad I listened to Father.

In 1985 we bought Mick's share and Joyce and I decided to build a house on the land which has splendid views down to the River Tamar. It is right opposite the Lodge where we lived before and we call our new home Clements. It is named after Clements Well that is situated on our land.

In the past Mother used to walk down from their home at Trenear via the lane to Woodlands because there was no entrance to our ground from Cotehele road as there is today.

Mother carried a peck-basket filled with pasties and other food to last us all day. She worked alongside my father, my adopted sister Joyce and myself and our workman Stan Harris, especially during the busy periods. We grew a lot of gooseberries, red, white and black currants, raspberries and strawberries, which kept everyone busy from dawn to dusk. I still have some of the old type tubs that were used to send off raspberries for jam making back in the 1920s and 30s. Father brought them down with him from Mount Pleasant so they are over 70 years old and antiques now!

Like all growers in the early days produce was sold at Devonport Market and taken from Cotehele Quay by the Market steamer. When I was 15 years old we acquired our own transport. Father bought a second-hand car from Gilbert Martin at Towell Farm and Bill Roberts up at the garage at Oak Tree converted it into a truck for us. The Roberts family had built a bungalow alongside Trenear around the same time as Father built his and the Roberts brothers had a workshop there where they repaired the villagers cars and machinery over the years. They had petrol pumps there as well until the late 1970s.

After we got our own transport we drove to Devonport Market, three mornings a week. That meant us all getting up at 3am to finish loading and get to Saltash to catch the first ferry of the day at 5am. There was always a crowd of vehicles waiting to catch that ferry as you had the best chance of selling your produce at a fair price if you were first to reach the market place. It also meant we could be home again by 8am to start the day job! It was hard work, but we were notoriously early risers as were my mother's sister Mary and her husband Nelson Mason and their family of Little Braunder of Halton Quay.

In 1936 we took delivery of 100 pittosporum bushes which Father had bought at the Bath and West show, which was held at Plymouth that year. This was the first pittosporum grown in the district. The majority of the pittosporum that is grown around here now originated from those few trees as Father grew hundreds from seed and sold the young shrubs to other potential growers.

Father had one full-time worker besides ourselves and that was Stan Harris from Horsepool near St Mellion. He came to Father straight from school and was with us until he retired. Except for a period during the war when he alternated weekly between us and Mr Johns at Dairy Mill and also took on a Post round at St Mellion, Stan spent all his working life with us.

When I was a youngster all the work was done by hand. Stan Harris and I spent most of winter skimming weed in all weathers. We had no waterproof clothing, we wore heavy hessian sacks over our shoulders and tied around our waist apron fashion. When they got saturated we had to change into dry sacks and carry on.

It was after Stan retired that Loveday's husband Mick Downing joined our work force. He came in 1955 and stayed for 19 years. In 1974 he left us and started work as a gardener at Cotehele House and later became head-gardener there until he retired in 1994.

Loveday had chosen not to work on the land she became a secretary with what was then St Germans Rural District Council and made that her career.

We were the first in the Parish to grow eucalyptus and it is now our main source of income. We started off with 100 bushes and we cut everyday. It is very quick to regenerate. The foliage has to be in perfect condition for market. Each piece the same length. We weigh every bunch to ensure uniformity and a bunch weighs 6oz. We have to pick in all weathers to fulfil our regular orders, but at least we have decent waterproofs to protect us. We sell up country through wholesalers and our produce goes all over England and Scotland. We once traced the destination of some of our eucalyptus and we discovered it was being used for window dressing at Harrods in London. We have a local customer from Harrowbarrow who has a regular order from us and she dries it for flower arranging. Recently a new group has been started up in Cornwall calling themselves Cornish Foliage Ltd. They have encouraged scores of growers to go over to eucalyptus and amateurs who have no experience in growing foliage have planted hundreds of acres. They employ pickers who are paid by piece-work so the standards drop as they try to increase their output. I fear for the future of the trade because wholesalers won't want the produce if it is not up to the mark. We have a young man Lee Clarke, who works for us part-time and has been coming since he was at school. He has been taught the proper way to do all the work and is very efficient now and can be relied on to do the job as well as we do ourselves.

At one period in the late 1960s we joined a newly formed group called Tamar Valley and Elburton Growers who used the trade name STARPACK. Although they would take everything we produced I was never very happy with them and felt we were just a number instead of an individual grower. They worked on the principle of fair prices for all which meant sometimes, that those of us who produced very good quality goods subsidised those who were less efficient. I felt it was the worst thing we ever did and I was glad to get out of that scheme after ten or eleven years. We are quite happy using our present arrangements.

We also grow a lot of pinks and my wife Joyce bunches most of them. Pinks can be grown in the same tunnels year after year providing we sterilise the ground before replanting they are pretty resistant though they do wilt sometimes for no apparent reason.

When the corn is ripe on nearby farms we get trouble with Thrips. These tiny insects can damage both the leaves and blooms by making minute holes in them so we have to be constantly on the look out and spray as soon as

Phyllis Rickard, Edie Rickard, Jane Veale picking gooseberries c.1954.

they appear. The plants have to be fed and well watered too of course. All this and the cutting of foliage has to be done by hand but we now keep the ground clean by mechanical means. I still have the very first cultivator we bought, a Colwood. Harris's from Ivybridge came and gave us a demonstration and we bought our first little rotovator for £40 and we thought it was wonderful. We have gone up market a bit since then.

We sell a selection of fruit, vegetables and flowers on a stall outside our house and pick up a lot of passing trade from car drivers on their way to visit nearby Cotehele House. Strawberries are always popular as customers know the fruit is fresh and well presented. However, not all our customers are so keen to pay for their purchases and we do loose a good deal of produce due to theft. We watch people sometimes. They are about to drive off then notice us and make the pretence of putting cash in our 'honesty tin'. When we check the tin later it is obvious they have just put in a few coppers instead of the correct amount. But we cannot spare the time to have someone on the stall, so we have to up our prices a bit to cover the losses like the shops do. Hard on the many honest folk who regularly buy our produce, but that is life today I'm sorry to say. But most of our customers are happy with what we sell and are willing to pay a fair price for fresh produce.

When our son Andrew, left school at 15, he decided he would like to join the Royal Navy. But there is no seawater in the Veale's veins and he didn't like the navy life and bought himself out for £20 after three months. He worked for us then until he married a farmer's daughter. Andrew went to live in their farm worker's cottage and worked for his in-laws, but sadly his father-in-law had a severe heart attack and had to give up farming. Andrew and his wife came back to St Dominick and took over the land and house at Woodlands which adjoins our ground. They now grow similar crops to us and use the same markets. Andrew's wife, Dawn is a wonderful worker, she loves outdoor work and is a great help in the business. They have two children, Gary and Karen.

Peter left school at 17 and he works for us and lives at the Lodge. He has three daughters, Lisa and twins Sarah and Claire.

Joyce's younger brother Joe Collins has had various jobs over the years, but he has always kept a market garden going in his spare time. His son Adrian rents fields near Fursdon and he is a

Fred Collins at Stockwell. A days work completed! c.1940.

Henry Collins picking 'Horace' at Stockwell c.1946.

Geoffrey and Sylvia Mason with best man Gerald Veale
September 25th 1947.

full-time market gardener. There are not many of us left in the business now. I'm pretty sure our boys will carry on the family tradition of market gardening. Things have changed since Father's day – we are now mechanised to a certain degree and polythene tunnels have been introduced over the years but we still work very hard.

Our women folk, like my mother, pull their weight and share all the work as St Dominick wives have for generations. I've always been happy doing market gardening and I don't intend to stop as long as I am fit. I'm nearly 75 but I still do a full days work. Lately we have had an occasional holiday abroad, which makes a change, but I'm always glad to get home as I find holidays are more tiring then a days work.

1922

Jan 2	'Darkies' called in evening.
Jan 7	Put up 'princibles' for motor-house.
Jan 24	Went to dance shaved my face first time since Michealmas.
Jan 26	Bought straw from Hockings 50/- cwt.
Jan 30	Planted 17 cherry gribbles in wood.
Feb 1	West Cleave not sold (withdrawn £925).
Mar 3	Went to Cosmopolitan Gym at Plymouth with F. Rabbage and A.Jope to see Ted Moore; Plymouth beat Pierre Nicolas in 4 rounds.
Apr 12	Miss McDonald died.
Apr 13	I grafted 50 Bramleys in the wood.
May 5	Calstock beat Bere Alston 1–0 at Tavistock in semi-final.
May 6	St.Dominick won the Bedford Cup at Tavistock.
May 11	Fred Rogers's car collided with a sailor on a bike near Saltash and killed him.
May 16	A big car came with petrol and I had 12 cans.
May 17	Fred Rogers attended Inquest.
May 24	Mr. Arscott told by Dr. he has a growth and Freeman Herring married.
May 27	Mr. Arscott died.
June 1	Mr. Arscott buried first one in new churchyard.
June 3	Went to Bath and West Show at Plymouth.
June 10	Miss Alma Vosper drove her car 1st. time.
June 19	Mr. Arscott's pony sold for £23.
July 13	Motored to market with 60 dozen chips cherries 5/- doz.
July 22	Cherries down to 3/6d a chip.
July 25	Cherry Feast at Pentillie Castle.
Oct 3	Kathleen Striplin married Sleep.
Oct 5	Killed first pig sold at £1 a score. (20 pounds)
Nov 11	At market, Armistice Day and in the midst of all the noise and bustle in the market a whistle blew and in a twinkling of an eye a dead silence for 2 minutes.
Nov 11	William Friendships banns called 1st time.
Dec 23	Bought 1/- oranges and 1/- nuts for Christmas.
Dec 24	Went to church and home and sang carols and hymns on gramophone.
Dec 25	Mary Snell and Duke came to dinner and M.S. played the mandolin and we all sang.
Dec 28	George Rickard and Lucy Reep married.
Dec 30	Mrs. Lewis Trenance died sudden 46 years old.

This very old picture shows Johnny Veale's wife, Alice. c. early 1900s.

Well-known couple, Edith (née Rashleigh) and Fernley Veale who lived at Vernigo. Edith was especially known for her support of St Mellion football club. c.1960s.

Fernley Veale, like many of his brothers, went to America in his youth. He returned with the American army to France in 1918 where he was awarded the French 'Croix de Guerre' medal for bravery. He spent six months in hospital recovering from his wounds. He was a market gardener until his death in 1967. Fernley and his wife, Edith, would be the great-grandparents of my daughter's children, Daniel and Matthew.

1923

Jan 4	Went to hear Burrows lecture on Temperance. Football committee meeting.
Feb 12	Frank Rogers took load to Plymouth in 'One and All' to hear Gypsy Smith.
Feb 18	3 Wagtails in my bedroom all night.
Mar 18	Saw two butterflies 1st time.
Mar 22	John Olver and Win Martin married.
May 8	Sown 3 rows Flower of spring broccoli then 5 rows of April Queen then 6 of Drumhead Savoy and 3 row Wroxton Brussel sprouts.
May 12	Cold enough for Christmas and I was told Mable Morrish (Rabbage) had a son during the week
May 13	Horace Jope and 'Look' Hocking wore long trousers 1st. time.
May 19	Our boys beat St Marks 5–1 and Mrs R Striplin died and gooseberries 5d a pound.
June 1	1st chip full of new potatoes for market. 3d a pound.

July 28	Frightful lot of starlings clearing the cherries.
July 30	Finished cherry picking through the starlings. Last cherries made 9/- dozen.
Aug 1	Duke went Callington Show and took 3rd prize in high jump Fiddler Reep took 1st in pole jump and Sambles 1st in the mile race.
Aug 14	Frank Brown left Congdons. Mary Snell goes Callington and bought a table, frying pan flue brush etc.
Nov 8	M.S. and Duke spend 1st night at Smeaton.
Dec 1	Apples made 2d. a pound, greens 1d a pound, turnips 2d each and pie fowls 9d a pound.
Dec 24	Cut a holly for Christmas tree and went Victory Hall in evening and Sam Vosper and Joe Trenance and all sang carols.
Dec 25	Lot of singers from Metherell called and we heard an earthquake rumble at the same time.

CHAPTER THIRTEEN

Hunter's Oak Garage

by Natalie Allen

Another example of the changing face of St Dominick was the closure in 1997 of a garage, which had served the community for over 70 years. Hunter's Oak Garage on the road between the 'Who'd of Thought it' Public House and Cotehele Quay, was first opened to service the solid tyred Model T Ford cars and trucks belonging to market gardeners and farmers in the village in the 1920s.

The first proprietor was the late Harold Newcombe and four years later, on leaving school William (Bill) Roberts became apprentice there. When Mr Newcombe gave up the business some three years later, Bill, although he was only seventeen years old at the time took up the challenge and decided to run the garage himself.

Over the next few years the local inhabitants purchased more vehicles as growers began to convey their own produce to the Railway Stations of Gunnislake, Kelly Bray and Saltash. The days of the horse and cart were over.

As the trucks were mainly used for this purpose, some owners only taxed their trucks during the spring and summer and laid them up as winter approached. This meant that in January and February, Bill was kept very busy making sure everyone's truck was roadworthy in time for the new season.

Most of the increasing trade came Bill's way and for some years his brothers Fred and George (Ambrey) became involved in the garage work before moving on to their own chosen professions. They all became familiar with the more sophisticated cars and the changing scene of motoring.

The arrival of the early mechanical cultivators in the 1930s brought another aspect of engineering to the little garage and Bill was kept busy repairing and servicing these new additions for the market gardening fraternity.

Here again Joe Snell's diaries give an indication of their unreliability in the early days of their manufacture. Joe tells us that he bought his 'Auto-Culto' on 16th July 1931.

Hunter's Oak Garage. c.1999.

Two months later on 16th September his diary states: *'Roberts came down to right auto-culto 1/-'*. 22nd September *'Started to use auto-culto in strawberry piece'*. But within a day the mechanic was called in again. On the 29th, *'W Roberts brought me down a plug for auto-culto'*.

Since the arrival of the modern equipment, there didn't appear to have been much work actually achieved in Joe's garden and I got the impression Joe wished he had carried on digging by hand and never set eyes on this 'new fangled' bit of machinery. However, on 13th November, Joe bought some galvanise from Biscombes of Callington and made a shelter for said engine, after which there was little mention of the machine until 7th March 1935, when once again the expertise of a motor mechanic was called upon.

'Roberts down about the auto-culto', states Joe.

On the 12th Bill called again and two days later yet another visit was requested. This time the repair was quite technical as Joe writes, *'W Roberts replaced 2 'doings' on auto-culto'*! A little later, *'Roberts had to adjust starting handle'*.

It seems that Joe did his bit to make the Robert's garage a thriving concern, but no doubt Joe's machine was not the only one to provide work for Mr Roberts.

The provision of petrol pumps provided more custom and the hand operated pumps serving Pratts petrol were kept busy as more and more cars and motor bike owners used the facilities of the garage.

The garage like the village Post Office became one of the focal points in the village, where local gossip and the state of the produce markets were discussed.

During the late 1930s the Roberts family built a bungalow alongside the garage and next door, Mr Ethelred Veale had an almost identical home erected and the Veales and Roberts were neighbours for many years. Bill's widow still resides there.

The garage was very much a part of the village scene and Bill and his helpers could turn their hands to anything mechanical. However, ill health meant that Bill Roberts had to retire in the 1960s, thus ending a forty-year involvement for the Roberts family. Soon after this petrol sales ceased, but the business continued to provide a local service, being run for some years by Kevin Hayes and from 1994 until its closure, by Stuart Gladstone trading as Alextone Autocraft.

Now only the rather dilapidated building survives, standing as a sad memorial to a bygone age.

Wesleyan school pupils at play at 'Well' corner. *c.* Late 1920s.

CHAPTER FOURTEEN

The next person I called upon was able to describe another aspect of market gardening. Francis Steer was a salesman for the Dutch bulb firm Van Zanten and he sold anemone corms to growers in the Tamar Valley and beyond for over 50 years.

Once again I was interviewing a member of the Langsford clan. Francis's grandmother, Emma, was my grandfather's sister which means, that Francis and I are related along the way.

Francis's story is both interesting and informative and I am sure you will enjoy sharing his memories and the family photographs he and his wife Ethel kindly allowed me to publish.

St Bridget and De Caen

by Francis Steer

Francis Clarence Steer. c.1998.

My name is Frances Clarence Steer, but a lot of people call me Frank. I was born in 1916 and brought up at Treragin Farm with my sister Gladys and two brothers, Ronald and Denis. Gladys died last year aged 78, Ronald is 75 and he lives in Bridgwater and Denis is ten years younger than I am. He married Edward Rickard's daughter, Doreen.

My parents were Harry and Florence Amelia Steer. My grandparents were Nick and Emma Jane Steer *née* Langsford. My gran used to spoil me a bit as she always took me with her when she visited our relations. Gran would never wait to be invited; she just turned up on the doorstep unannounced! She thought nothing of walking from her home at Treragin on the road to Harrowbarrow, to visit Uncle Harold and Aunt Dorothy at Stockwell or even her brother James at Birchenhayes. I don't remember visiting Birchenhayes as a child but I used to love going into Stockwell on Sundays to play with my cousins Harold and Jim Maunder.

In 1930 my grandparents sold the farmhouse, buildings and twenty acres of land for £1,000. They moved to a nearby house with eight acres of ground, that they already owned and after our parents died, Denis and I each took over a part of that land. Denis built a bungalow and put up greenhouses and went into market gardening in quite a big way. His daughter and son-in-law built a bungalow there too and have taken on extra land. They have put up tunnels, packing sheds and a cold storage room and she has gone into the floristry business and makes wreaths and bouquets. I kept my share of the land until 1994.

I married Ethel Medlin in 1942. She is one year younger than me and we have one son, Nick and two grandchildren. When we first married, we lived at Treragin for a year. Then we lived in a house at Tamar View until we built our bungalow in the village.

I started off in a small way. Times were not good when I was a youngster and there were four of us children to feed. My first job was working as a gardener for Mr Hoskin at Cotehele Quay. I stayed there for five years, but the money was poor. I was getting twelve shillings a week. I had a bit of a sideline as I kept poultry and worked a bit of ground for myself.

Then I got a job driving for Mr Fred Rogers. This was during the war and at that period Mr Rogers had a food depot at his stores and this food had to be distributed to various towns and cities. I drove one of the four lorries and I went to Plymouth, Bideford, all over the place. I made deliveries at Princetown prison and trustee prisoners used to help me unload the provisions from my lorry. I recall they were not issued with butter, but had low-grade margarine and were rationed of course the same as everyone else. The prisoners used to beg for cigarettes, but I never gave them any, as it was an offence to provide them with anything. My lorry was searched before I was allowed out through the prison gates to ensure no one was attempting to escape.

The other drivers were George Downing, William (Bill) Searle and Ronald Fry. Owen Rogers and Fred Baker also worked at the store. Everyday, produce was taken from local growers to Saltash station to be sent up country by rail and I often drove that lorry.

Then one day I picked up a man who wanted a lift. He said he worked for a Dutch firm and was trying to sell anemone corms in the area. He was a Londoner, but was an agent for Van Zanten of Holland and he asked me if I would be interested in the work. I agreed to try and do some selling, so he introduced me to his boss who was also over here and I got on very well with him. The other chap wasn't really keen on the job and he soon gave up. Mr Van Zanten came to see me and he was very pleased with my sales figures and he asked me if I would continue. That was in 1944.

When anemones were first introduced to West Country growers, they cost £2.10.00 (£2.50) for a small 2,500 packet, but after a year or two, as more Dutch men came here selling corms, the price dropped considerably to nine shillings per thousand. They gradually increased in price over the years and at the peak period of sales they cost £4.50 per thousand (in decimal prices). They are now a lot more expensive at £7.50 per thousand.

Tony and Val Van Zanten and Diana, Ethel and Francis Steer and Nicholas in Haarlem Holland. c.1954.

Holland is very suited to growing anemone corms as the soil is sandy and weed control is easier. The seed is sown in early spring and by the time the corms are harvested at the end of the summer, they are large enough to sell. Anemone corms are graded into four sizes and measured in centimetres. There are 4-5s, 3-4s, 2-3s and 1-2s. We sell the 2-3 size commercially, as they are more productive than the larger sized corms.

There were a few other Dutch salesmen around at that time, but we had the run of Devon and Cornwall and our corms were very good quality and sold well. Mr Van Zanten dealt with the Cornish sales and he had a lot of big customers down in Cornwall. We had some 5000 customers in all. I took on the Devon side and at the peak of the anemone boom I sold four million corms in one season. That was a lot of anemones! We sold some double flowered St Bridgets, but most of our trade was the De Caens type. I had a wonderful business going around Dawlish and Exeter and I did a tremendous amount of trade around Calstock and Bere Alston. There were over twenty growers in the Kelly area at Calstock, all big producers. I could go to Calstock of an afternoon and sell 100,000 corms with no trouble. The 1950s were the peak period.

If I went there today I'd have a job to sell ten thousand. Everybody, just everybody, used to grow anemones then; even the farmers put in a few thousand to supplement their income in the winter months. But there came a period when farming was a thriving concern. Cattle, sheep and milk were all selling well, so farmers felt there was less need to grow anemones. A lot of the small market gardeners were also giving up their land as they reached retirement age and many areas which had been cultivated for almost a century were being given over to conifers. The anemone trade began to die out as a result.

To produce the best crops, anemones need to be grown in fresh ground each season, and then they can be a very viable winter crop. We recommend high percentage potash manure for high flower production and you can't beat blood, fish and bone meal as a good all-round manure. Anemones are pretty disease resistant, but there were problems at one stage when flowers developed very curly foliage, which spoilt their appearance. This has largely been overcome as the Dutch growers did some experiments. They discovered that instead of selling the corms as soon as they were harvested, they held them over for twelve months and the trouble diminished.

At one time growers here experimented with the practice of leaving the corms in the ground for a second season, but it was not successful commercially, although a few corms in your garden might well come up and flower year after year in the right conditions.

At one time I had a field, out behind the village playing field and we grew a marvellous crop of anemones out there. I remember Myrtle Northcote out there with my wife picking anemones when the ground was white with snow. The plants look fragile, but they are very hardy and survive frost and most other winter conditions.

After my bulb business began to do well I gave up my job at Fred Rogers, but I kept on a field out Treragin way, where we grew daffodils and strawberries.

Ethel worked very hard over there bunching and picking flowers, but I also employed six or seven women during the busiest times as I couldn't get on the ground much myself as I was spending so much time on the road selling corms and tulip and daffodil bulbs. I was lucky because Aydon Langsford always let me have a fresh piece of ground for my anemones each year. I had only a few acres of my own, but using Aydon's ground I could plant up to 100,000 corms a year and they did well. We produced excellent crops over there. I sent a lot of flowers to the florist, Anne Stephens in Drakes Circus, Plymouth. I had a problem finding time to get the produce down to Plymouth two or three mornings a week when I was so busy and away so much. I was friendly with Sidney Dawe up Trehill and he had a shop in Plymouth. He kindly offered to take my flowers to Plymouth any time and that was a wonderful help. He did that for me until he retired and it was very convenient.

We had a television in our home at Bohetherick in time for the Queen's Coronation. At that time Anne Stephens didn't have a television, so on Coronation Day she and her family came up to our place for the day to watch the ceremony.

Ethel and I got to know Tony Van Zanten very well and in 1954 we were invited to their home in Haarlem in Holland. We had a wonderful fortnight out there with our little son, Nicholas. They took us all over Holland and into Belgium. We visited Brussels and Antwerp and the war cemetery at Arnhem. That was sad, but it was wonderful to have the opportunity to visit it. They gave us a really good time and we have a photograph to prove it!

We had a terrible trip back across the North Sea. I shall never forget it. The weather was shocking, it was that bad I was surprised they ventured out to sea that night, but we made it back to England and all was well.

For eleven years we lived in the row of houses alongside butcher Tom Martin's home Trigg. Ethel worked for Mr Charlie Northcote before she married. He was a tailor and had a little shop next door to his home. It is still there, but is just used as a storeroom now. Mr Northcote was a bachelor until he was over 70 years old, then he married a widow Mrs Mary Parken. He had some ground at Fursdon and that is where Ethel worked. He was very good to her. Everyone had a bit of ground and sold their surplus fruit and vegetables at Plymouth market. Two acres was considered sufficient to provide a living for a man and his family and employ a man to help with the work. They even managed to retire on what they made out of a piece of ground that size. They had to work hard in those days.

I bought my first car; an Austin 7, in 1939 and I gave the equivalent of £12.50 for it. I kept it for a year and it went well and never cost me a penny in repairs. Then I thought I ought to have something a bit better, so the chap who sold me my first car, went to Plymouth with me to look round. I saw a Standard, which I fancied, but they wanted £100 and I couldn't afford that, so I went for an Austin for £40. I had it for twelve years, then one day it broke down at Milehouse and I had to get a garage to collect it and repair it for me. The repairs cost me £50, so I decided it was time to get rid of it. I went to Mumfords to buy a new Austin A40, but they didn't have one for sale, only an A50 which was bigger and more expensive. I asked if they would buy my old car, but they said no, but offered to put it in the show room window for me and if it sold, all well and good. So I took up their offer and within a day or two a lady bought it for £150 so that was a very good deal. I decided to go for the A50 then and it did me very well. I have done fairly well with my cars really. Ethel decided to learn to drive this new car and she was doing very well, but one day she stopped going up over the steep hill from Cotehele and the car started to run backward. She eventually pulled it to a stop with no damage done, but she lost her nerve after that. I only bought one new car and that was a Nissan. My present car only had 4,000 miles on the clock when I bought it, but its fifteen years old now and still going on all right.

I used to buy my petrol at Fred Rogers when I worked there, but the nearest garage now is in Callington.

In 1959 we heard that Mr Jim Reep was selling off building plots on the road opposite the football field. We decided to buy a site and we hoped to get the first one next to the allotment field, but Norma and Chucks Chapman were also interested and they had been given the choice of two sites. We kept our fingers crossed and we were delighted when Norma chose one further down the road. We bought our larger site for £350, which included an extra fifty feet of frontage. We had our bungalow built and moved in the year that the Tamar road bridge was opened in 1961. We had the first two bungalows that were built alongside the main road, but dozens of bungalows have been built further down into the village since then. The original road hedges were demolished and the whole area opened up. We love it here; we are not bothered by anyone and have lovely views across the fields towards Devon.

Our only son, Nick was not interested in market gardening. He is a sound technician with Granada Television. We often see his name come up on the credits. He is mostly involved with drama, but has travelled all around the world in the course of his job. He married an American girl he met at college and they have two children. Benjamin is in his third year at Oxford studying physics and Juliette is specialising in chemistry. We are very proud of them both, but we would like to see more of them. They live in Manchester because that is where Nick's job is.

I think our generation will be the end of an era. Youngsters look much further afield than their birthplace for their livelihood these days.

I gave up our land at Higher Treragin about five years ago, Ethel had to slow down a few years ago for health reasons. My field was alongside St Dominick Holiday Park. Although it is called a holiday park, the sixty odd chalets are occupied by families on a permanent basis and the owner also has similar projects in other parts of the country.

When I was thinking of giving up our field, this gentleman made me an offer of a lot of money and I thought to myself I would never make that much cultivating the field, so I accepted his offer. He has since built a house on the site for his son.

I had been selling anemones and bulbs for fifty years and seen out three generations of the Van Zanten family in that time. That family concern has been taken over by another Dutch firm and so last year I decided the time was right for me to retire. Anemones are still grown in a small way at Landulph and a few other places, but the boom years are over. Now I just have our own bit of garden to cultivate, but there are a couple of rows of anemones thriving amongst the vegetables in my back garden.

1924

Jan 4	For market, 2 rabbits 1/- each, 4 fowls 4/- each, 3lb sprouts, 3d per lb.
Jan 11	A Jope, V Traise, W Collins and I and D Wadge went down by Dick's car to the Cosmopolitan Gymnasium to see Tex G Roukes's white hope, Isaac Ingleton of Nottingham 6ft 3 in, 14 st age 22 beat Bombs Landsberry, Champion of India, 6ft, 13 st age 27 knocked out in the 4th round.
Mar 5	Mr H Reep, Trenances, L Nattle, P Bridgeman went to Scilly Isles.
Mar 20	Bought Caster meal 10/- cwt. Fish Guano 15/6 cwt.
Mar 24	Went to meeting at Victory Hall and I am appointed one of the trustees.
Apr 21	Frank Rogers and I had evening trip down to Trenances and Vospers, Reeps and F Rogers gardens.
May 1	Took car to Halton Quay for 5 cwt coal.
May 7	Took 3 boxes flowers up to catch G W R motor (cost 1/-) and brought home 12 cans of petrol from F Rogers.
May 24	I bought a pair of Whippet Tweed trousers 17/6.
May 28	News of Mr James Langsford's death.
May 31	At market and saw Queen of Romania and Lady Astor MP in Fore St Devonport who afterwards visited Cotehele House.
June 5	Fixed up some scarecrows in the strawberry ground.
June 23	Boy Pengelly came strawberry picking 1st time and we picked 191 chips.
June 25	Children down for flowers for their service and A Snell bunched over 500 gladioli.
July 1	Motored to Devonport with 415 chips of strawberries (2 lb.) and sold for 1/- chip.
July 3	Motored to market with 515 chips a proper glut – made 10d chip.
July 26	Harry and I had our photo taken. Went Hatt sports.
Sept 18	G Langsford removed Mr J Braunds furniture from mill and took it to Symon's at Cotehele.
Sept 25	Young Taylors and Mrs arrived in his car with ducks and tools 1st time.
Sept 26	New neighbours moved into mill.
Oct 7	Renewed motor licence £4.10.0 ordered pair boots off Mart Rickard and young Taylor gave me a packet of 50 cigarettes for lending hand with furniture.
Oct 8	Goose fair did not go first miss for about 25 years.
Nov 20	Mr R Langsford and Miss L Martin married.
Nov 22	Balsom took over Frank Rogers's car, 'One and All'.
Dec 1	Balsom took 'One and All' up Smeaton 1st time.
Dec 11	Went up Frank Rogers for 4 cans petrol and paid 11/4 for same.
Dec 29	The 'One and All' having overhaul at garage and young Roberts started learning.

St Dominick Football Team

Back row: Lewis Trenance, ?, Eric Martin, Dick Wadge, Tom Johns, Ned Gorman. *Middle row:* Percy Nattle, Lewis Reep, Bill Turner, Parson Square, ?, Wendell Channing, George Channing. *Front row:* Ronald Rickard, Frank Rowle, ? (with ball), Albert Reep. c.1921.

CHAPTER FIFTEEN

Like the Post Office and the village Pub Fred Rogers's store was a meeting place for local growers. Weather conditions, prices and crops were discussed whilst delivering produce to the haulier and buying new supplies of chips, manure and sundry goods. Bulbs were dropped off for sterilising, advice sought and given and all the local gossip exchanged. The store was a hive of activity and played a major role in the production of fruit and flowers in the Tamar Valley in the heyday of market gardening.
Here now is the story of Pitt Meadow and the stores, as told by Fred Rogers's youngest son, Vivian.

Pitt Meadow Memories

by Vivian Rogers

Three generations of my family have had the privilege of living in St.Dominick during a 100-year period of the most intensive industry the village has ever known. My ancestors were living here in the 1600s and possibly before.

My grandfather, William Henry Rogers was born at Ashton in 1862, one of eight children. It was he who saw the beginning of the boom in market gardening in the area. He left Callington School at 11 or 12 to screen tin at the Prince of Wales mine and then had various occupations including coach driver to Canon Hullah of Calstock.

In 1887 William Henry Rogers married Selina Jane Striplin, whose parents, William and Elisabeth Striplin lived at Pitt Meadow. William Striplin built Pitt Meadow in 1842 on land leased to him by the Earl of Mount Edgcumbe for £6 per annum. The leasehold was for two lives and after their deaths the house and land returned to the Earl.

Fred Rogers's fleet of lorries on the store forecourt. Note the headlight restrictors, which were compulsory on all vehicles during the war. c.1940.

The 1881 census recorded William Striplin as a market gardener and there were 22 punnet and basket makers listed. Selina, aged 19, was listed as 'garden help to parents' and her older sisters as 'stand-in market'. No doubt the sisters enjoyed their outings down river by steamer from Halton Quay to Devonport market, taking their garden produce for sale. Several families made punnets in their homes during the winter evenings.

By this time the trees on the steep valley slopes had been felled and the scrub cleared, largely by ex-miners who would otherwise have been out of work when the mines closed. This land could now be cultivated. Grandfather was cultivating the land at and around Pitt Meadow, thus starting his market gardening career. He rented land at Fursdon to keep a pony for working the land and also hired out horse, cart and driver for 5/10d per day. One day his brother, Jack, reversed his horse, 'Warrior', too near the tip at Smeaton Quarry (the present site of my brother Terry's bungalow), it went over and the horse had to be shot and it's remains left in the quarry.

In 1904, the farm tenanted by Walter Lawry at Bohetherick was split up and Grandfather rented a field there for 35/- per acre, but due to heavy demand, this was soon increased to £6 per acre.

My father, born in 1890, was not expected to live and was simply called 'Fred'. Fred left St Dominick School at 13 and joined his father market gardening and driving a horse and cart. In 1909 Fred and his older brother William, ran a wagon in the Cleave Valley and Mash Road, collecting fruit to meet Bonds wagon at Pitt Meadow. If the wagon was full, they would take the produce direct to Saltash station. In 1910 the brothers took over Perry Spears Agricultural business at Halton Quay. Punnets were made there and coal that came up river by barge was delivered in the village. By 1913 Rogers Bros. had eight horses, mainly taking fruit to Saltash station. Some of the fruit was sent to jam factories in Truro and Gloucester.

Fred Rogers married Edith Mary Martin, from Heathfield Farm in May 1913 and my sister Vera was born at Pitt Meadow in 1915.

By 1916 father's health had broken down, and he could not work in the agricultural mills. At the outbreak of the First World War, the War Tribunal ruled that he should run the business and William was called up. Fred became too ill to carry on the business and it was sold to Plymouth Co-op, but he retained the haulage business and in 1917, he took over the Bohetherick gardens from his father. He was also building up his Horticultural Merchants business at Pitt Meadow.

William Baker Striplin had built a large carpenter's shed, where the lawn at Pitt Meadow is now and it was here that wooden flower boxes, fruit boxes, sections etc., were made and stored. An

Where the business started. Shed at Pitt Meadow where wooden flower boxes were constructed. Note the Euonymous shrub on the roof which, was grown and shaped by Vivian's grandfather. Vivian demolished this shed when he was a teenager and the area became part of Pitt Meadow lawn. c.1920s.

Two pound chips of strawberries being loaded for the station. Meadow building.
Left to right: Herbert Martin, Terry Rogers, Fred Baker, Fred Collins, Henry Collins, Fred Rogers, Joe Collins. *c.*1950.

office was built adjoining the house with a petrol pump outside. I can remember selling petrol at 1/2d per gallon. Father also rented two large stores in the Goods Yard at Saltash station. The horticultural business expanded after the war to cater for the increase in market gardening, every bit of available land was being used at that time.

My brother Terry was born in 1921 and I arrived in February 1924. We were then living at Pitt Meadow in the northern end with our grandparents in the other part of the house. Grandmother died there in 1928 and my grandfather continued to live there until his death in 1946.

By this time, lorries had replaced horse and wagons and during the 1926 Strike, Father drove a Ford lorry to Covent Garden in London, loaded with Double Whites. Quite a journey then.

At this stage in his life my father was already engaged in what was to become, a lifetime of public work. He was Chairman of St Dominick Parish Council for many years, Chairman of St German's Rural District Council, and at the same time was Worshipful Master of Loyal Victoria Lodge of Freemasons.

He served on Cornwall County Council for many years, eventually as Vice-Chairman. He was Chairman of the Governor of local schools and a Governor of Seale Hayne College. He was Chairman of Callington Magistrates; (later my brother Terry took over that office and Vera was Chairman of Saltash Magistrates). He was Chairman of the County Hall Committee and Ellbridge Horticultural Experimental Station and served on many other committees. All this involved travelling to Truro several times a week. (No subsistence or travelling expenses then).

By the 1920s daffodils had become an important crop in the area, but bulb eelworm played havoc with plantations and could remain in the soil for many years. The eelworm, too small to be seen with the naked eye, would bore into the centre of the bulb and kill it, then proceed to adjoining bulbs killing off whole patches as they went. However, two scientists, Staniland and Beaumont, had discovered in the laboratory, that eelworm could not survive in temperatures of 110°F and over. But a commercial method had to be found to heat the centre of the bulbs to this temperature. Father, who was by then a leading Horticulturist in the south-west, was asked to help. He provided the facilities in a galvanise shed at Pitt Meadow. A second-hand boiler was purchased from a tin mine to raise steam and then blow it into a treatment tank of water.

Picking *Double Whites*
at Pitt Meadow allotment.
Edith Rogers, Fred Rogers,
Emily Tink, Owen Rickard,
Liz Read, Fred Baker,
Terry Rogers, Vivian Rogers.
*c.*1928.

After several experiments, a satisfactory method was devised where the bulbs would remain in a tank of circulating water for 3 hours at 110°F. It was discovered that a higher temperature would kill the bud within the bulb, whereas a lower temperature would not kill off the eelworm. Now, amazingly, some seventy years later, this is still the only commercial method to kill bulb eelworm. We provided this Hot Water treatment of bulbs for growers from the 1920s until we retired in 1985, putting through many hundreds of tons. Father would often light the boiler in the early hours of the morning, get up steam, heat the water and put in a load before breakfast, then go on to Truro to meetings. My grandfather would then be left in charge of the treatment. It was hard work for about six weeks in the summer, when growers had lifted their bulbs ready for the treatment prior to replanting. After the Second World War, we built a new plant in premises at Meadow Buildings. This boiler was oil-fired and later we had electric hoists and pumps, which made it the most modern plant of its time. For some years we treated bulbs for the Rosewarne Research Station at Camborne.

Other pests and diseases were prevalent and had to be dealt with as best as possible, with the limited range of chemicals then available. Gooseberries were dusted with lead

Fred Rogers, Fred Baker and Edmond Symons, loading wooden flower boxes at Pitt Meadow.
Boxwood sections, raffia and a ball of twine are in the foreground. *c.*1920s.

arsenate and sulphur for caterpillars and mildew, I can remember seeing my father mixing these with bare hands. Tar oil was used on fruit trees. Bullfinches (Hoops) would cause a lot of damage to gooseberry buds and were shot in quite large numbers. They were killed as far back as the 1820s when growers were paid 2d per bird from the Church rates! The killing, but not the payments, continued until the last war.

Around 1930, one of the first greenhouses in the village was erected at Pitt Meadow. Tomatoes and early daffodils were grown. Bulbs were planted in boxes, left outside for a few weeks, then taken inside to produce an early crop. Water was piped down from a stream into a storage tank, then pumped onto the crops with a ratchet pump. Mother would spend days boxing the bulbs in a shed especially built for the purpose by Richard Striplin. She would also spend long hours in the gardens, picking fruit, weeding etc. Father bought two old buses and converted them into packing sheds and my mother used to bunch flowers there, using raffia before the advent of rubber bands. With Father running the merchants business and attending meetings, Mother practically ran the market garden. Women made a great contribution to the success of the market garden industry.

In the years before the war many acres of fruit were being grown, which resulted in a surplus. My parents looked for more outlets and decided that canning could possibly be the answer … They purchased a machine and tins and had very attractive labels printed, depicting the river and Brunel's rail bridge. They made a success of it and were preparing to purchase larger equipment when the Second World War was declared. There was no longer a surplus, as during the war there was a ready market for fruit.

Father gave up the tenancy of Bohetherick field in the 1930s, to concentrate on his merchants business, but retained the fields at Pitt Meadow. In 1938 he bought Pitt Meadow house and it's grounds, land at Cross opposite the Butcher's Arms, (now the Who'd have Thought It.) and also the quarry at Smeaton. A store was built on the one-acre site at Cross and this became known as Meadow Buildings. Many years previously, this site had been earmarked for a new school, but the scheme fell through. Our petrol pumps were moved from Pitt Meadow to the new site and the new hot water treatment plant was installed.

Fruit punnets and baskets had not been made locally for many years, but were factory made at Irlam in Manchester. We purchased these in large quantities and they were delivered by rail to Saltash or Callington station. Cardboard boxes had replaced wooden ones for flowers and these were obtained from Goughs of Norwich. These were sold with all other sundries from our new warehouse. Our telephone number continued to be St Dominick 2.

A lorry load of produce bound for Birmingham market during a rail strike. H Buckle, T Rogers and village children. May 18th 1954.

September 1939 came and with the war the pattern of growing changed. The flower acreage was cut annually by 50% and replaced by vegetables. Some daffodils were planted in hedges and can still be seen there today. Double Whites were almost eliminated as they were not a reliable cropper. There was a ready market for fruit, 'jowlers' coming from as far away as West Cornwall to buy our crops. This resulted in a considerable reduction in our merchants business including transport. We then took on another job. We stored tons of margarine, lard etc., that was on ration and delivered to retailers in East Cornwall and West Devon. We extended our warehouse to 16,000 sq. feet and in the new section stored 2,000 tons of ground Rock Phosphate, (Sahara Desert sand), from which the Phosphate is extracted for fertiliser. This was kept in reserve and not used until after the war. The Ministry regularly sent an Inspector to check the sand. On one occasion, he decided we must have a fire extinguisher! We painted some buckets red and filled them with the sand. On the next visit the Inspector was quite satisfied! Whenever there was a heavy night air raid on Plymouth, Father would disperse the lorries in nearby lanes in case of a direct hit. Bombs did fall on Mash Lane and Towell Farm.

After the war market gardening continued to thrive. New varieties of daffodil bulbs were imported from Holland and distributed by Fred Rogers Ltd. New varieties of strawberries were introduced and anemones became an important crop. Glass cloches were used extensively to produce early strawberries, then came polythene cloches and later, walk-in tunnels. A new range of efficient chemicals came into use and machinery improved considerably. All this resulted in a large increase and variation in sundry sales. During the period March–June 1968 we carried 120,000 packages of fruit and flowers to Plymouth station. By this time British Rail had ceased collecting freight from Saltash, Calstock and Bere Alston stations, so we were also collecting their produce and taking it to Plymouth for despatch. We noticed a considerable drop in the number of packages when wholesalers decreed that daffodils should be sent whilst in tight bud. This meant that as many as 60 bunches could be packed into one box as opposed to the more usual eighteen or twenty bunches when the blooms were fully open.

Terry Rogers, Ernestine Cradick, Vivian Rogers, Marion Cradick. c.1930.

During the war, Fred Rogers Limited, ran a tractor contracting service, which started with a Ransomes caterpillar tractor and progressed to the Ferguson tractor. This service continued for many years.

The 1970s saw the decline in market gardening for various reasons. Our distance from the main markets was a severe disadvantage, British Rail were no longer able to get the produce to its destination in time for the early morning market. Fruit had to be marketed locally and this saw the start of the 'Pick your Own' trade. Road transport was provided for flowers, with our warehouse as the loading centre. The quality of anemone corms deteriorated and therefore were not so widely grown. The steep, labour intensive slopes were no longer viable. Daffodils were now being grown for bulbs as well as flowers, which involved lifting the bulbs every two years, which meant the use of more sophisticated machinery.

The import of produce from the Mediterranean, indeed from many parts of the world, was the final straw. This hit the greenhouse growers as they had the disadvantage of rising heating costs.

In the 1970s, we opened a Garden Centre in part of the warehouse, but our main business was to serve the commercial grower.

Alderman Fred Rogers with his wife and daughter Vera at Buckingham Palace for the presentation of his OBE. c.1958.

Vivian and Terry Rogers on the forecourt of The Meadows. *c*.1985.

A few years after the war Terry and I had become Directors of Fred Rogers Ltd., with our father. He retired in the 1960s, but still took a keen interest in the firm. In 1958 he was awarded the OBE, which he richly deserved, for services to Horticulture and the Community. Mother and Vera accompanied him to Buckingham Palace for the presentation by the Queen. Father had built a bungalow called Meadowcrest on land, which he owned at Radland, and he died there in 1974, being outlived by my mother, who died five years later. Terry and I retired in 1985, the warehouse was demolished and bungalows built in its place, leaving no trace of the 47 years of intense activity on the site.

The one hundred years of intensive market gardening has turned full circle, the steep slopes have been returned to trees and many of the gardens returned to grassland. However, there are a few very productive and expanding nurseries in the village who have found a niche in the market and are growing high quality produce.

I have been fortunate in spending most of my life in St Dominick and experiencing the many ups and downs of market gardening life.

Born at Pitt Meadow in 1924 I grew up with my sister Vera and brother Terry who was born in 1921. We all got on well together despite the nine year age gap between us. Vera although having different interests looked after us well. My school days started at St Dominick Lower School and I remember the morning of my seventh birthday when my teacher came into the classroom and said, "Vivian, I shouldn't leave that bar of chocolate on your peg in the classroom."

"Please Miss" I said, "It isn't mine", but up jumped a lovely five year old with long fair hair and said "Yes Miss it is Vivian's I have just given it to him for his birthday". I do not know who was most embarrassed at the time, but last year that little girl and I celebrated our golden wedding.

As a small boy I spent much time looking for marbles in the garden at Pitt Meadow, these had been brought there with the dock dung from Devonport. The marbles had been swept up with the dung which, was loaded on to barges and taken up river and used on the gardens as fertiliser. This practice ceased in 1913 as it was deemed unhygienic.

From St Dominick School I went to Callington Grammar School and then to the Hoe Grammar as a boarder, until the bombs started falling precariously close. I then had an old motor bike, which I rode to Saltash parking it in Father's store in the Goods Yard. One night the store was blown up with my books inside. The school was burnt down by incendiary bombs, so I studied at home for Matriculation and passed satisfactorily. During one of my holidays, I demolished the carpenter's shed at Pitt Meadow. The ground was laid out to lawn but the well, which supplied our water, is still there. We had another well behind the garages and it was from there that we pumped water to a large storage tank at the top of our house. This was pumped using the old hot water treatment boiler to raise steam and work the pump. This pump can still be seen working at Dingle Steam Village at Lifton.

I have never forgotten my first driving experience at seventeen. We had a converted Austin 16 pickup, which I drove to Brentswood to collect flowers. The track was very narrow with a steep drop on one side and turning involved a good deal of skill. I was always fascinated at Brentswwod watching the plough or other implement attached to a wire rope, being pulled up the steep slope with a winch fitted to a stationary car at the top of the hill.

After school days I took a horticultural course at Reading University and then joined the Ministry of Agriculture on food production.

Vera had married John Morley Tamblyn in 1935 and had two children Judith and Mark. Terry who had joined the RAF married Joyce Congdon of Radland Farm in 1942 and also had two children, Hilary and Angela.

Grandfather died in his sleep in 1946 and was one of the last of the parishioners to have a walking funeral. I can still picture him in the shed making wooden boxes and stitching sections for fruit boxes, or if helping with the hot water treatment of bulbs, sitting on an up-turned oil drum keeping an eye on the steam gauge and thermometer. In the evenings he would sit by the fire reading the paper and smoking his pipe. Often on Saturdays I would fetch his tobacco from Em's shop at 10½d for one ounce of Black Jack and collect tripe from butcher Martin's and my children's newspaper from Charlie Northcote at his shop in Bohetherick.

In 1952 father bought Radland Farm and sold off two fields to Westlake Rickard and George Finch. The farmhouse and fields were sold, but we later bought back the fields, which I used for market gardening with the help of Owen Rickard, Sam Medlin, Geoff Steer and Bernard Hatch. Strawberries, raspberries, daffodils and anemones were the main crops with much of the fruit being taken to Newquay shops.

Fred Rogers's 'store' at St Dominick demolished for house building. c.1985.

In 1948, I married my childhood sweetheart Marion Lucy Herring of Bohetherick Farm at St Dominick Church. Marion has been a wonderful wife for over fifty years. When we married food petrol and clothes were still on ration and furniture was limited to the Utility Range when we moved into Tor View. In 1951 our daughter Carolyn was born. The three of us moved to Pitt Meadow in 1955 and our second daughter Sally Joanne was born in 1956. Marion made a lot of improvements in the house at Pitt Meadow. In 1970 she skilfully planned the acre garden and laid it out to shrubs and lawn, just in time to erect a marquee on the lawn for Carolyn's wedding. Joanne and Lawrie also had a marquee on the lawn for their reception. The garden has given us much pleasure and we enjoyed hosting church fetes and various Garden Parties for charity. We did have our opportunity to attend a Garden Party at Buckingham Palace, the similarity being shortage of parking space!

Carolyn and Nick have presented us with three grandchildren, Natasha. Lisa and Edward. Joanne and Lawrie with two, Nicola and Christopher.

After retiring in 1985 Marion and I enjoy walking and I have continued my interest in Amateur Dramatics with Prim Raf and Rif Raf and also bowling. On reaching 70 I retired as Chairman of the Tax Commissioners.

In 1992 we decide to prepare for old age and moved back to Tor View after living at Pitt Meadow for 41 years. We renovated and extended Tor View and sold Pitt Meadow. This was the first time it had been out of the family since my great grandfather built it in 1843.

Last year Marion and I celebrated our Golden Wedding and we are now happily settled at Tor View with frequent visits from our daughters, grandchildren and many friends.

1925

Jan 15	Mrs Taylor Radland Mill a daughter.
Jan 21	Lecture to village hall on bulb growing.
Jan 26	I brought home cross-cut from Striplins and Ern cut my hair.
Feb 3	Went to village hall to hear Abbis speak on horticulture. Showed him a flower to see if he knew the name, he did. ORNITHOGALUME from Africa.
Feb 25	Taylor's started to clean a piece of ground below coach drive.
Apr 18	Saw 1st swallow.
Apr 20	Heard cuckoo 1st time.
May 10	Charley Langsford, Birchenhayes and his brother and wife down Mrs Arscotts to tea.
May 18	Mrs Arscott and Amber went off in morning and returned late 10.30.
Aug 18	Gave Mary Snell £2 for Wimley (*Wembley*) tickets.
Sept 24	Mr R Striplin put new bridge at Radland Mill.
Sept 28	New people arrived at mill. (*Davey*)
Sept 29	Spent day at London Exhibition.
Oct 1	Picking plums.
Dec 7	Taylor's brought home the 'One and All' 1st time.
Dec 9	J Taylor 1st trip to Callington.
Dec 10	1st trip to Plymouth with 'One and All'.

1926

Feb 15	Went to football dance a record crowd and a good time. Duke and Lil Maunder won spot waltz prize.
Feb 21	W Downing little girl christened Geen (*Jean*).
Mar 16	J Taylor went Martin's sale and bought pump etc.
Mar 23	Striplin started to build Taylor's motor house in village.
Mar 27	Mrs Willis Kelly received her false teeth.
Apr 13	Frank Rogers found a heap of old clay pipes out Spur House.
May 4	Papers full of General Strike.
May 6	L Reep, N Striplin and others motored to London with flowers.
June 2	J Taylor brought home 25 cartridges for me, 5/3d.
Sept 3	Taylor's had wireless fixed.
Oct 14	J Snell Ashton summons find (*Fined*) £1 for disobeying police.
Nov 1	Old Mr Taylor died in evening.
Nov 17	Paid Newcombe 3/6d for bulbs for motor lamps.
Nov 19	I phoned Dustan Callington and he came and put in a set of new tremblers and a new plug and put the car going proper 15/-
Dec 21	I cut ivy and laurel for Xmas market. A poor market.

CHAPTER SIXTEEN

On my first visit, Tom Gorman assured me that he knew nothing of importance, but on subsequent visits, as usual, an interesting tale began to unfold.

Out came the photo albums and once again a little more of the village history was brought to life for me. Tom is very proud of his old home and I was invited to view the entire property. The oldest part was very quaint, with low ceilings and uneven steps leading to different rooms. The staircase in this part of the house is made of stone and curves in the style of a 16th century pole staircase. The stone has been carefully encased in wood over the years for greater comfort, but it seemed to me that this might well have been a servant's stairway to the upper floor. The walls and ceilings are of the original lath and plaster and it is very easy to believe that the house has been in existence for three centuries. In the yard are the remains of a large stone-built shed, which in the Grill's time had housed their steam engine and threshing machine. Pastoral scenery and a quiet location in the village make Fursdon an idyllic retreat for Tom, Chrissie and the family cat!

Fursdon

by Tom Gorman

Fursdon is over 300 years old and my family have lived in this farm house, since 1902. That is when my grandparents Thomas and Emma Jane Vosper, *née* Lampen came here with their four daughters, Helen, Min, Ethel and Alma.

I am related to the Langsfords because my grandfather's, sister Mary Vosper married Charles Langsford the miller and they had thirteen children.

Tom Gorman's grandmother, Emma Jane Vosper. c.1930s.

I am Tom Gorman and I was born in 1916. My parents were Edwin (Ned) and Helen (Nell) Gorman *née* Vosper.

We lived at Bohetherick in the first cottage in the row opposite Em's shop. Our neighbours were Lily and Albert Wadge. I had one sister, Nesta. We attended the Wesleyan School but I hated school. I would go off all right in the morning, but after dinner I'd kick up and wouldn't go back. Mother used to chase me all the way up the road with a stick and Nesta used to ignore me. She was older than I was and she was disgusted by my behaviour. My mates were Hedley Vanstone and Alfie Striplin and we always played together. Alfie and me used to mitch peas from Sam Poad's market garden on our way to Sunday School. One day he lay in wait in his packing house and caught us and we got into big trouble over that.

Prior to 1902, the Grills family lived here and the farm was a lot bigger then. They also had a threshing outfit and kept their machinery and engine in a big shed in the farmyard. When they left, the Edgcumbe's let about 30 acres to the Council for allotments. Those fields just up

The three Musketeers! Alfie Striplin, Hedley Vanstone, Tom Gorman. c.1921.

Tom and Nesta Gorman. c.1921.

Chrissie Hill (Gorman) c.1938.

Four year old Maxwell O'Dowd with his great-grandfather Thomas Vosper. c.1934.

Alma Vosper c.1920s.

Ethel Vosper c.1920s.

the road from the farmhouse were let to various tenants in lots of one or two acres. They have always been cultivated by local people, but not many villagers want to work on the land these days. Adrian Collins and Mike Searle have taken most of them over now and work there full-time.

When Grandfather came here this was a large family house. During the 1930s it was made into two homes but it still has doorways linking the properties both upstairs and down. My two aunts, Ethel and Min Vosper lived in the right hand section, which is the oldest part of the house. There were large meat hooks in the kitchen ceiling over from the days when the Vosper's sold meat from there.

Aunt Ethel remained a spinster, but Aunt Min married Jim Wakeham and they had one daughter, Kathleen. Their marriage broke down, so Aunt Min and Kathleen continued to live at Fursdon. Kathleen married Norman Lodes and they kept a garage in Callington in later years. They had two children Barry and Rosemary.

Aunt Ethel and Aunt Min worked very hard all their lives. They took over some Fursdon land and did market gardening. They employed a couple of men at peak times and they were the first in the Parish to grow Snowdrops, commercially.

My sister Nesta married Alwyn O'Dowd who was in the Navy. When he left the Navy he worked an allotment for quite sometime and grew pittosporum, anemones and spring flowers. They had one son, Maxwell and Max was the village milkman for 28 years.

When Grandfather died in 1938 he was 86 years old. That is when I took over Fursdon. I did some market gardening and we had an orchard. I reared store cattle, but never did dairy work.

When I came here to live over 60 years ago, I was paying £1 a week rent for the farmhouse, outbuildings and 33 acres. I gave up the fields in 1990 and they were put with neighbouring Haye Farm. I only rent the house and outbuildings now, but I don't dare tell you what the Trust, the present owners, charge us today! Property was very cheap to rent when I was young and there wasn't much point in owning a house then, but if we had bought the house back in the 1940s it would have been worth a great deal now.

Tom Gorman in his 'pinny' with father Ned Gorman and Emily Martin, outside Em's shop at Bohetherick. c.1918.

In 1942 Grandmother died and that year I married Chrissie Hill. Her parents were Stan and Olive and she had one brother, John. They lived in a little bungalow in Foxy Park at Halton Quay, where they worked three or four acres of ground. John did not marry, he later moved to a cottage at Halton Quay and has recently died.

We have one daughter, Jacqueline. She lives at Lostwithiel and has two daughters and two grandsons.

Chrissie can remember Dick Floyd who delivered groceries for Attwoods in Callington. There was no need for a car in those days; everything was delivered to the door. In later years the Co-op had a travelling shop which sold groceries. Butcher Congdon called regularly, as did Langman's bakery van and the milkman.

My first means of transport was a motor bike that I bought from Bert Rickard when he was called up during the war. It was a Velocette and I gave £63 for it and had it for years. Bert and his wife Phyllis lived down Quarry and he was a mechanic.

At one time back in the 1980s the television presenter Fern Britton lived here and we all

Wilfred Martin and young Tom Gorman in the garden behind Roundy Cottage.

Wesleyan Chapel Sunday school group

Back row: Vera Medlin, Kathleen Gorman, and Marjorie Wadge. *Front row:* Maurice Rickard, Vera Rogers, Phyllis Medlin, Winnie Wadge, Aileen Reed, Hedley Vanstone, Alfie Striplin, Tom Gorman (sitting) Ronald Martin. Tom does not know why he and Hedley were wearing those titfers! *c.*1921.

became very good friends and her mother used to visit us too. We are still in contact with them.

When the new council houses were built at Trehill Cross my parents left Bohetherick and went up there to live, but both of them and my grandparents died at Fursdon. Father died in 1956 and my mother ten years later.

Chrissie's parents died within three weeks of each other in 1974.

We are very content here and I hope that Chrissie and I will keep fit enough to be able to spend the rest of our lives at Fursdon.

Nell Gorman. *c.*1958.

Max's Mysteries

May I suggest that if at some future date, someone in the village decides to compile 'A Stitch in Time' Mark 111, that the very first person they interview be Max O'Dowd. Max got a mention earlier in this book, but it was not until my book was already at proof-reading stage that I spent an hour with Max at his request. I left his home with a mixed bag of memories and mysteries which I had little hope of solving in the short time available before my final deadline. How I wish I had spoken with him much earlier, thus allowing myself time to explore more fully the incidents he described.

How could I fail to be intrigued to learn of the presence in Radland Wood of the grave of a gypsy? Max had discovered the gravestone whilst playing in the woods as a youngster, but could not recall the inscription or indeed the exact location of the stone. What hopes did I have of finding it some sixty years later?

Another mystery, which must be left, unsolved, is the tale of Hospital Point or Hospital Pool, as it is sometimes known. As a young teenager, Max and his mate Alwyne Rickard used to go salmon fishing with Stan and George Langsford, off Cotehele Quay. Listening to the fishermen's conversation, Max often heard Hospital Point mentioned. Over the years it has been said that at some period in the past there was an isolation hospital built in the woods at the far end of Dynas Town Lane within easy reach of the river, hence the name of this particular point on the River Tamar. No proof has been found as yet, of the presence of this hospital, but what a strange tale and one worthy of further investigation.

Max O'Dowd's maternal grandmother Nell Gorman *née* Vosper, lived at Quarry and at that time according to an 1882 O S map there were other cottages nearby which have since been demolished. As a very young child, Nell attended the 'Penny School' which old maps show to have been situated on the corner of the lane leading from the hamlet of Burraton to Burcombe Farm. Pupils paid one penny a day to attend this school. This was prior to the erection of a schoolroom behind the Wesleyan Chapel in 1871.

During the 1939–45 war when gun emplacements occupied the field alongside Smeaton Quarry, Max and his friends spent hours coasting around the village lanes on their bikes, looking for shrapnel and other wartime souvenirs. On one such occasion, Max was in the lane below Roundy Cottage at Bohetherick (Courtney Vanstone lives there now) when he spied some disturbed ground inside a gateway. On further investigation he discovered a concave metal object and began to dig around it with his bare hands. After a while old Mr. Bill Roberts looked over the gate and said 'Look boy, there's a load of soldiers up the top of the lane and they have just put up a notice saying 'Danger unexploded bomb'. Max realised then just what he had found and ran and told the soldiers who came down and dug out the bomb, which had landed upside down. The Bomb Disposal team were given a drink at the pub after completing their task. Max recalls seeing two bombs lying in a truck with a chap guarding them. The soldiers jokingly told him that he deserved a drink too, as he had done half the job for them! The bombs were taken to what was then a dump at Smeaton Quarry (Terry Roger's bungalow now stands on the site.)

Max watched from a safe distance by the school and heard an explosion and saw a large plume of black smoke. After a suitable time he went up to the quarry but the soldiers had left the site so presumably both bombs had been disposed of safely, but Max has often wondered since why there was only evidence of one bomb exploding. Max reckoned he had a lucky escape that day. Some sixty years later it is hard to believe that St Dominick played its part in the defence of the Country during the war. Guns, searchlights, the Home Guard and American soldiers camped in farmer's fields, these are all still remembered by the locals and many a tale remains to be told … but that's another story.

1927

Jan 1	Went to market by 'One and All'.
Jan 31	Cut 10 bundles of willows.
Feb 5	Duke's went to Dick Wadge's place to hear wireless.
Feb 14	Went to village hall to hear lecture on C Dickens by Peacock, Saltash.
Mar 7	Went to village hall to hear Mr Jim Lawry age 87 give lecture on League of Nations.
Mar 26	Kelly Bray water works opened.
Apr 13	Stranger fishing. (*Was this Houdini as recalled by Mr Taylor*)?
May 13	Paid £20 for 4 cwt Ornatus bulbs.
May 22	Horace Jope and Miss Renfree's Banns called 1st time.
June 4	For market 6½ dozen red gladioli 1/-, 3 dozen Brides 2/-, 6 dozen yellow daisies 6d, 17 dozen cabbage 1/9d, 4 dozen rhubarb 1/9d all per lb., 136 eggs 1/- per dozen, 27 chips strawberries 2/6d each, 84lb. gooseberries 3½d per lb, 2 tins cream at 6d, 2lb butter at 1/6d, chicken 1/3d per lb, iris 6d bunch. (*Sending produce to market or up country everyday via Kelly Bray station*).
June 6	Horace Jope married.
June 29	Eclip (*Eclipse*).
July 7	Cherries 4/- chip (12lbs) Cullins 2/- white hearts badly cracked by rain 2/-
July 23	Miss Alford and I parted.
Aug 19	Vet came and looked at my pig and didn't know what it was.
Aug 23	Swine man came to examine pig.
Aug 25	The Police came to know if we have heard anything more about pig.
Sep 1	Man came and killed little pig to find out its trouble. Peritonitis.
Sep 5	Phyllis Duke goes school first time.
Sep 21	Mr Davey left Radland Mill.
Sep 27	A J fined £1 for not sounding his horn at cross roads.
Nov 2	Went Callington and bought 5 Charles Ross 2/6 each, 10 Ellison's orange 2/6 and 10 Lanes Prince Albert 2/- each.
Nov 3	Received wire from Heard not to kill pig, glut on market.
Nov 4	Planted apple trees in Berry Orchard.
Nov 8	Went to village hall to hear Freeman lecture on Agriculture research.
Nov 9	Killed 1st pig Heard paid me 7½d per lb. for pig.
Nov 25	For market, 4 pigs and their belongings! Paid 7½d lb. Fowls 9d per lb., potatoes 5/- cwt. (*all through autumn pigs weighing from 129-149 lb. each were sold*).
Dec 23	Blanch Martin (*Langsford*) died.
Dec 26	White snow and we spent day like Sunday. Snow drifted by hard wind feet deep in places and blew down apple and pear trees by lake.
Dec 27	No Postman owing to snow, no cars running.
Dec 28	Blanch Martin buried.

James Rickard, tailor and outfitter, billhead c.1904.

Ladies Cricket Team: Mabel Herring, Vera Studden, Zena Langsford, Georgie Sambles, Joyce Veale, Francis Reep, Winnie Parken, Front Row: Topsy Parken, Margaret Searle, Elaine Rickard, Joyce Finch and Jean Rickard.

CHAPTER SEVENTEEN

Trenance is not a name you are likely to hear mentioned in St Dominick today, yet in the pre-war years the name was as familiar as Grills, Northcote and Vosper. Times have changed. Gone are the butchers, tailors and bargemen, who made their living in the village and gone too, are these family names which once featured so widely in the Cornish hamlet of Bohetherick.

By the 1860s, one John Trenance had fathered six sons and two daughters. Two sons moved away from the Parish, but the other young men lived and worked in Bohetherick and the name Trenance, became synonymous with the growing of plums and other tree fruit in the Tamar Valley. Their gardens were notorious, with acres of fruit blossom each spring, adding to the beauty of the spectacular view of the River Tamer where it sweeps between the marshes, on its way to Woodlands and Greenbank Farm and on past Halton Quay.

Of the Trenance brothers who remained in St Dominick, three had children. Lewis had three daughters, Leone, Muriel and Irene. William and his wife had one son, but he died when he was sixteen years old.

James had a daughter, Marien and a son, Edgar, who left the village when he grew up. On the death of Miss Marien Trenance, in 1989, aged 91, the family name died out in St Dominick.

When I decided to include the Trenance family in my book, I had to visit Lewis's grandchildren, Alwyne Rickard, Jean Laing and Nigel Hunn.

I am grateful to Alwyne and Jean for their contribution and the memories their tale evoked. The mention of the Chapel Anniversary reminded me of an amusing incident. It was the usual practice for my family to attend the anniversary service at Landrake Chapel on the first Sunday in May. Our Aunt Ethel Congdon lived at Landrake, and she always invited all the family members to her home for tea

Lewis and Minnie Trenance lived in this picturesque cottage. It later became the home of Ronald and Aileen Fry and is now known as Oakfield. *c.*1920s.

on Anniversary Day. One year, the preacher chose as his topic for his sermon the expression, 'No two alike.' I listened with interest when he explained that in nature nothing was really identical; not even two snowflakes were alike or no two people either. That was his theme and it was both instructive and entertaining. On the last Sunday in May it was the day of Trinity Chapel's anniversary which my mother, sister and I always took part in. By coincidence the preacher was the same gentleman who had preached at Landrake and to our amusement, he preached exactly the same sermon! But that was not the end. When, at a later date, we attended Bealbury anniversary service, the same thing happened again! I hope he did not recognise us in his congregation. 'No two alike,' indeed!

My sister and I did not attend Sunday school, but we usually joined the villagers for the annual Sunday school outing. Two or three coaches were hired from Watsons of St. Ann's Chapel, and Torquay, Paignton or Newquay or some such seaside resort, the usual destination. All the teenagers would occupy one coach on their own, so that their noisy sing-songs and giggles would not annoy the older generation, most of whom preferred to travel in a more sedate manner. Sunbathing, swimming, and games on the beach was the normal ritual for the children, whilst the grown-ups had a welcome tour of the shops. Ebenezer Chapel also had an annual outing and most people attended both trips. Holidays away from home were almost unheard of in the village sixty years ago and these two days trips, were the highlight of the year. As a child, my mother attended the Wesleyan school, which was opened in 1871, walking everyday from her home at Jubilee Cottages. The children used to play in the road outside the chapel and go down Towell Lane to drink from the well down there. No 'busing' or hot school meals in those days. My parents were married at St Dominick Church, but both my sister and I were married at the chapel. My two daughters were christened there, but the chapel was demolished before they married and their services were held elsewhere.

Kathleen Martin of Towella took a series of photographs showing the demise of the chapel in 1991 and some are included in my book. The chapel held so many memories for local people. Kathleen also unearthed copies of the hymn sheets used at the Sunday school anniversary services and I have reproduced one of them, as a momento of yet another part of village life that has joined the realms of history.

I am grateful to Nigel and Wendy Hunn for providing old family photographs and my thanks are extended to Jennifer Graham, whose colour photographs depicting the modern-day work-force at Sunningdale Nurseries, have added so much interest to this particular chapter of the Trenance family history.

Tuneful Memories

by Jean Laing

My name is Jean Laing and I have a brother Alwyne, and a sister Elaine. Our parents were Ronald and Leone Rickard, *née* Trenance. Our great-grandfather on our mother's side was John Trenance. He had six sons, Jack, Ernest, Joe, William, James and Lewis and two daughters, Bessie (Striplin) and Emma (Hughes).

Jack and Ernest moved away from the Parish when they were young men, but Joe and William rented ground on the slopes facing the River Tamar near Cotehele, which became known as Cherry Garden. The Trenances rented this land from the Mount Edgcumbe Estate, from 1900 till 1947. They planted hundreds of plum and cherry trees on these acres, but most of the trees have died out over the years and the land now produces eucalyptus and daffodils and the present tenant is Norman Searle.

Joe Trenance lived at Tamar Villa and he was considered to be a confirmed bachelor, but when he was in his seventies, he wed a young local schoolteacher, Miss Laycock. James married Edith Symons and they had two children. For some time prior to the First World War, James and his family lived at Brighton in Sussex where James was Captain of a pleasure steamer. However, during the war his boat was commandeered by the War Office and he was detailed to carry troops across the

Lewis Trenance tending his pear trees at Eastdown. c.1928.

Channel to the war zone. After the war ended, the family returned to live at Bohetherick and James joined his brothers on the market garden at Cherry Garden. Their son Edgar moved out of the village when he grew up and later became a Bank Manager at Padstow in Cornwall.

James's daughter, Marien did not marry and in later years she lived at Towell Cottage and took a great interest in the nearby Wesleyan chapel, as did most of the Trenance family over the years. Marien was the last person to bear the family name and with her death in 1989 at the age of 91, the St Dominick link with the Trenances, died out.

William Styles Trenance married Polly Martin and they lived at The Lodge at Bohetherick. They had one son, Harold, who died when he was sixteen. After his wife's death, William remained at the Lodge and Myrtle Nothcote kept house for him for eighteen years, till he had to go into a nursing home. He died in 1951, aged 89.

Lewis Trenance was our grandfather and he married Beatrice Newcombe. They had three daughters Leone, Muriel and Irene. Lewis Trenance was Captain of a Tamar barge in his early years and it is said that when his second daughter was born, Cap'n Lewis named her Muriel after seeing the name on a barge during one of his trips. When the barge traffic died out Cap'n Lewis changed hats and became a gardener like his brothers.

He planted up the six and a half acres of land known as East Down, which is situated just a few yards along the road from The Lodge. This area had a wonderful view of the Tamar, but was on high ground and open to the elements, so he erected wooden windbreaks at intervals and planted hundreds of plum trees. Daffodils also flourished there. He also worked a three acre field in Burraton Lane, called Poundwell Field. The bungalow where I live with my husband Bert overlooks this field.

On 30th December 1922, Lewis's wife Beatrice, died suddenly when she was only 46 years old, leaving three daughters, the eldest being 22 years old. Nine months later, Lewis married a local widow, Minnie Wadge who had one son, Albert. When Lewis's three daughters married they all married young men who were working for their father on the land. Leone married Ronald Rickard and they were our parents and they had three children. We never knew our real grandmother of course and Minnie Trenance was always known as our gran and we called her son, Uncle Albert. Muriel married Francis Hunn and they had one son, Nigel, who is himself, a grandfather now. Irene married Harold Harris but they had no children. In 1935, Lewis Trenance built two houses, side-by-side, for Muriel and Irene on land that he owned near Oak Tree. Our parents lived in what were then, the new council houses at Tamar View in the Burraton area of Bohetherick. I left school at fourteen and kept house for years, because our mum was ill for a long time. Sadly she died in 1954 when she was 54 years old. Ten years later, our dad married Roy Clarke's widow, Winnie. Our father died in 1980, aged 79.

When Grandfather retired the Harris and Hunn families took over at East Down. Nigel still rents the land from the National Trust and it is planted out to strawberries and bulbs. The trees our grandfather planted have all died out. Our father took over Poundwell Field, where he had always worked. This ground was always very well maintained and Grandfather used to say he could walk over his land and not find enough weeds to fill his waistcoat pocket. Grandfather employed one workman, who spent all his working life with him. Henry Striplin was first employed on board Cap'n Lewis's barge and when the river work ceased, Henry joined the work force on the market garden. Dozens of men and women were employed by the growers on a casual basis at peak times. The gardens were very labour intensive, wages were low, but there were always men and women

Jean and Bert Laing's wedding. *c.*February 4th 1952.

Back row: Frances King, Gilbert Rickard, Sylvia Rickard, Frances Hunn, Walter King, Glen Kellow, Joyce Finch, Valerie Kellow, Fred Rickard, Alwyne Rickard. *Front row:* Pearl Launder, Muriel Hunn, Nigel Hunn, Bride and Groom, Leone Rickard, Ronald Rickard, Elaine Rickard, E Rickard, Millicent Rickard, Bill Launder.

Harold Harris, Nigel Hunn, Jean Laing, Roy Clarke, Christine Cundy, Francis Hunn, Winnie Clarke. c.1956.
Courtesy of *Western Morning News*.

looking for work. After the flowers and strawberries were picked there were raspberries, gooseberries and currants to harvest and the men-folk would be picking tree fruit. Hundreds of people worked on the Tamar Valley gardens in the first three or four decades of the 20th century.

During the 1939 war, my brother Alwyne worked for Sid Mutton at Strip Haye Farm for a time, then he worked alongside his father. My sister Elaine used to help at Poundwell until she married Graham Tucker from Saltash and moved to Andover. Elaine has two children, Gary and Karen and four granddaughters, Sarah, Louise, Lauren and Lucy.

When Father retired in 1966, Alwyne and his wife Millicent took over Poundwell and they worked it together for twenty-five years. Alwyne and Millie have one son, Paul, but he had no ambition to follow in his father's footsteps, his career is in music and he is Lay Clerk at St George's Chapel, Windsor.

Alwyne sold his produce to Marquands at Polhilsa at Kelly Bray, and the produce was sold to shops in various towns in North Cornwall. They gave up Poundwell in 1991 and Roy Clarke junior now works the land. But Alwyne did not retire, he still works most days for his cousin, Nigel Hunn at their Sunningdale Nurseries, driving over from his home in Harrowbarrow.

The Hunn family still makes a living off the land just as their forefathers did a century ago. Nigel has taken over several fields in the Bohetherick area and he and his wife, Wendy, and their two sons, Darren and Ian, still grow acres of daffodils and have numerous tunnels planted to winter crops. They sell bulbs and also breed turkeys and chicken for the Christmas market. They import flowers from Guernsey everyday and these are made into bouquets by their helpers and then sold to garages and stores over a wide area. It is somewhat ironic that the Tamar Valley now imports flowers when for generations they themselves had been one of the leading producers in the country.

I married Bert Laing in 1952 and he spent his working life as a mechanic, first for Glover & Uglow at Callington and in later years for Harold Pascoe's haulage firm. Bert has no real connection with market gardening, but we always rented an allotment nearby and we only gave it up a few months ago.

After Mum died, I worked for my uncle, Harold Harris at East Down during peak times, but I became allergic to the pollen or sap in daffodils and I had to leave. In 1973 I joined the staff at Fred Rogers's store at The Meadows. I enjoyed that job, as I was in daily contact with local people, especially when the garden centre was opened. I stayed there until 1980.

But our life was not all work. We, as a family, always attended chapel regularly, that is where we joined with other local families in worship and song. Trinity chapel was built in 1868, on land donated by 'Brewer' Martin from Towell Farm. Our family had a strong association with the chapel and I was very sad to witness its demise in 1991. Bert and I were married there and it was always part of my life. Since our chapel closed, Bert and I have attended the Methodist Chapel at Callington, where we have been made very welcome.

Until the late 1970s, I am not sure of the precise date; our chapel always held its Sunday school anniversary services on the last Sunday in May. When we were children the chapel was always well attended every Sunday, but over the years, as people found other interests, the congregation gradually dwindled until, by the time the chapel finally closed it's doors there were only about 10 regular worshippers. In early years the chapel was lit by oil lamps and in winter oil heaters were placed in the aisles. Before electricity was installed in 1953, the organ had to be pumped manually

Francis Hunn, Christine Cundy, Millie Rickard, Jean Laing, Wendy Hunn. c.1965.   Courtesy of *Western Morning News*.

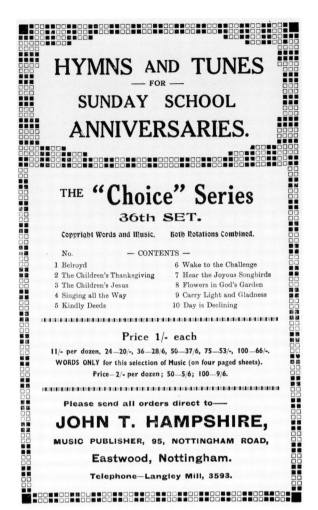

and over the years that task was undertaken by Courtney Vanstone, Alwyne Rickard, Clarence Capon, Joe Collins, Nigel Hunn and Fred Behennah. Organists I recall include Jack Langsford, Kathleen Gorman, Marion Gibbs, Ronald Rickard, Paul Fry and Jill Rickard. By the mid-70s, the Sunday school attendance had fallen and that is why our Anniversary services were abandoned. But when I was a child and a teenager Anniversary Day was one of the highlights of the year. Two services were held on the Sunday, one in the afternoon, when even the tiniest child took part and another at 6pm when the chapel was filled to capacity. When the pews were filled, chairs and forms were brought in from the schoolroom behind the chapel and the congregation then filled the aisles. Many of these people were from the Ebenezer Chapel at the Churchtown end of the village and also from chapels much further afield. Every little wayside chapel held such services and we all supported each other. Preachers were chosen from other parts of the Circuit and they were invited to a member's home for lunch and tea on the Sunday.

On this special day the Choir and Sunday school pupils entertained the congregation with special hymns. Weeks before the day, Sunday school teachers spent hours teaching the little children all the new hymns and the choirmaster tutored the older members and made sure they were note and word perfect, in time for Anniversary Day. All the Trenances and Vospers had very good voices and the chapel was noted for its lively singing.

On the day before the service, male members would erect the platform, on which the choir sat facing the congregation. Strong trestles and planks were set up and long forms put in place. Everything had to be very secure, as over forty singers were seated on the platform and it was quite a hard task getting everything into place. Of course all this had to be removed when the event was over and a number of men were relied upon to do this each year. After the men had completed the platform, the women members gave the premises a special clean ready for the occasion. When Anniversary Day finally arrived what excitement there was!

The menfolk wore their best suits and all the ladies and girls had new dresses and hats and it became quite a fashion show as each member vied, in the nicest possible way, to out-do her neighbour. Our mother could not afford to buy Elaine and me a new dress every year. Sometimes we wore the same frock two years in succession, but with new trimmings on our bonnets and a few other refinements, I doubt if very many people realised that we were not *quite* the height of fashion! In those days, hats were always worn when attending chapel, unlike today, when the sight of a hat is a rarity. Ribbons, flowers, artificial fruit and feathers, all put in an appearance atop each smiling face and the whole effect was very colourful. Some members were more daring than others and each year everyone wondered just what creation would appear. Ascot had nothing on Anniversary Day at St Dominick!

On the Monday following the 'big day', everyone enjoyed a wonderful tea party. Jack Langsford from Newhouses used to donate strawberries for all the children and members provided

The latest tying aid. Wendy Hunn at work. c.1992.

Ian Hunn packing daffodils. c.1992.

Alwyne Rickard retired! Helping out at Sunningdale Nurseries. c.1992.

Harold Harris. c.1992.

Nigel Hunn and Elizabeth Tink unloading imported flowers. c.1992.

A serious moment for Vera Duke, Audrey Stidwell and Kathleen Martin. c.1992.

Allotments at Oak Tree. In the background, Robert's Garage and bungalow. The end bungalow was Mr and Mrs Ethelred Veale's home until 1978. c.1992.

sandwiches, saffron buns and tufts with butter or jam and cream. The children ate first, then helpers would take them to a nearby field, where they had races and played games. The older members and visitors then had their tea, after which a final service was held.

One Christmas, in the 1950s we needed to raise funds for the Chapel and Aunty Muriel hit on the idea of transforming the schoolroom at the rear of the chapel, into a series of 'caves', each depicting a theme. The men put up wooden frames which were then draped with tarpaulins and divided into several small areas about eight foot square. Then groups of two or three people chose either a nursery rhyme, or perhaps a snow or woodland theme and proceeded to decorate their 'caves' appropriately.

```
St Dominic Ebenezer and Trinity Methodist Churches

                    Open Air Service

                          on

                    23rd July 1970

                          at

                    Cotehele Quay

                     7.15 p.m.

        Conducted by: Rev. Russell Pope
        Singing led by: Mr. W. J. Pomroy
          Items by The Dominiques
```

Some of the men were very enthusiastic and became quite competitive. One garden scene designed by Walter King had a working model of a miniature waterwheel complete with stream, mossy banks, trees and flowers. Another was Miss Muffet with a realistic spider hanging over her and Bert's contribution was a fully working miniature fun fair. Everyone paid a great deal of attention to detail and we helped each other out by supplying various items. The electricians and carpenters amongst us had to stand by at all times in case of a breakdown and we spent many hours working on our own special schemes. After a lot of effort and a few tears of frustration the displays were completed. One of our members, Mabel Finch was very skilled in the art of butter sculpture and she created an amazing floral scheme made entirely from butter. There were indoor and outdoor scenes and with masses of greenery and special lighting the effect was magical. Practically the entire village came to see our 'caves' and all the children were invited into Santa's grotto and given a small gift. We stayed open for three nights and visitors came from miles around. We produced Caves for four or five consecutive years and everyone declared it a great success.

Our Harvest Festival services were wonderful too. In my early years and into the 1950s and 60s, practically every farmer and grower would join in this service of Praise and Thanksgiving and the chapel would be full. The best of their produce was given to the chapel and the scent of ripe apples and fresh vegetables filled the air. All the window ledges were draped with autumn tinted creeper and large vases of seasonal flowers filled every available corner of the building. Tall pampas grasses were arranged on either side of the altar rail and the traditional sheaf of corn, donated by a local farmer and a large harvest loaf were set in place. The lively hymns and the singing of so many men made it a very joyous occasion. On the following Monday a harvest supper was followed by the auction of all the produce, the proceeds being donated to a chosen charity. The last Harvest Thanksgiving at Trinity chapel was in the autumn of 1989. The service took place in the schoolroom, as part of the ceiling in the chapel was unsafe. It was very sad to see our beautiful chapel demolished and it was the end of an era.

Around 1947 a group of men formed the Trinity Singers. The Trenances had good voices and they married into musical families. My dad, my husband Bert, my brother and my Uncle Francis were in this group. The Trinity Singers were Ronald Rickard and Alwyn O'Dowd, bass, Bert Laing and George Finch, baritone. The 1st tenors were Francis Hunn, Ronald Fry and Bill Gorman and 2nd tenors Albert Wadge and Alwyne Rickard. They performed at concerts in chapels all over the district and always sang on special occasions at our own chapel. Bert and I have also sung for many years with Freda Brown and her daughter, Jill, who also accompanied us on the piano or keyboard. We called ourselves 'The Dominiques' and we travelled as far afield as Hayle in Cornwall to Barnstaple in Devon. We entered talent competitions and won holidays at Butlins, where we sang to the holidaymakers. It was a wonderful period in our lives and we all enjoyed the events and literally travelled thousands of miles over the years. We still perform on occasions, but try not to travel too far from home these days. Jill is a very accomplished musician and composes music for various Shows every year. We are, at present, practising for a production of the musical 'Joseph and his Technicolor Dreamcoat', which is due to be presented in the Callington Circuit next March.

We are all very keen on singing and of course Alwyne's son Paul is carrying on the Trenances's musical tradition.

Our Uncle Francis was always known locally as 'Tucker' Hunn and he told us that this nickname came about because he couldn't swear properly when he was a youngster! 'Tucker' was as near as he could get to something worse! We never discovered why our Uncle Harold was called 'Boxer' Harris. He certainly did not have any connection with boxing when we knew him, but maybe his ancestors did.

Tucker Hunn and Boxer Harris were friends all their lives. Not only did they marry two sisters; they were partners in their market gardening business at East Down. The two couples lived in adjoining houses near Oak Tree, and there was even an interior door, linking the two properties. Uncle Francis died suddenly on 12th March 1970, which shocked the whole family. Aunt Irene was ill for some time before her death in 1979 and Aunt Muriel passed away in 1980. Uncle Harold continued to work with his nephew at Sunningdale for a number of years and he died in 1995 and their houses have now been sold.

But even in death the two families were not separated. They bought adjoining burial plots in St Dominick churchyard and they now rest side by side … together, as they had always been in life.

The demolition of the Wesleyan Chapel and Schoolroom. *c.*1991.

Demolition and Profanation. *c.*1991.

The beautiful screen behind the pulpit of St Dominick Wesleyan Chapel. *c.*1991.

The final service was held in Trinity Chapel Schoolroom in 1990.

Paul, Mary, Claire and Louise Fry; Bert Laing, Aileen Fry, Kathleen Martin, Winnie Rickard, Jean Laing, Joan Dyke, Rev. Peacock. Pianist – Jill Brown.

Television personality Fern Britton and Tom Gorman outside Fursdon. The door on the right is the entrance to Ethel and Min Vosper's old home. c.1980.

Ronald Fry admiring the strawberries grown by him and his wife, Aileen, destined for a Newquay Hotel. c.1960.

Rows of glass cloches and a spring scene at Aileen Fry's market garden at East Burraton. Aileen grew 'Gentians' in frames and these had to be sprayed with sequested iron or epsom salt to prevent yellowing of the leaves. She also grew 'Lily of the Valley' commercially. c.1960s.

1928

Jan 23	Our new people came to Radland Mill (Bennetts).
Feb 2	Sid Mutton and D Tarr married.
Feb 6	Finished planting Czars in Pond field and Phyllis goes home from school with measles.
Feb 14	Mr Martin Rickard (Shoemaker) had a stroke.
Feb 19	Mrs P Bennett (Shopkeeper) went through an operation.
Mar 4	Arnold Jope and I went to look at Treragin and meet Lewis Reep and Miss White.
Apr 3	W Worth drawn up 14 cartloads of dung.
Apr 15	Mrs W Trenance died.
Apr 30	Treragin sold for £1020 to a Mr Rendal.
May 10	Drove my car 1st time for a year and had 2 gallons of petrol off F Rogers and stopped at Sheffield to hear a Labour man talk.
May 24	Cabbage made 2/- 2/3 per dozen a good demand.
June 24	Edward Rickard and Jack Duke had their babies christened.
Aug 1	Went to Callington and bought 6 pigs L Rogers for 21/- each and 6 off Mutton (St Ive) 25/- each.
Sep 27	Jack Taylor's new car arrived at Newcombes.
Oct 2	J Taylor drove new car to market 1st time. Apples made 4/- per box of 60 lb. Beans 1/8 per 1000.

Oct 3	Went Honey Fair and measured for teeth and paid for same, and renewed motor licence and rode in with Luke and home with Ethel and Lez N.
Oct 6	My teeth arrived.
Oct 10	Went Goose Fair rode in with J Taylor and spent day with L Cradick.
Oct 17	Went to Callington and had my teeth 'put to rights'.
Nov 6	Kit Jope and Charlie Cox married and 'sweeped' the chimney.
Nov 10	Heard Duke's wireless 1st time.
Nov 16	Killed pig 144 lb.
Nov 17	For market, small apples and pears 4d per lb. Pig 7 3/4 lb., 'puddins' 7d, chittings 8d, liver 2½lb.
Nov 22	Today's news all football coupons to stop, illegal, to get 24 right 282 429526481 coupons would be necessary for to be certain 1 correct coupon. (*Worse odds than today's lottery!*)
Dec 3	Went Ashton threshing and went Victory hall lecture on gambling.
Dec 6	Finished planting pink spirea and killed 2 pigs.
Dec 8	New boots 21/6d suit of close (*Clothes*) Tozers 35/6d.
Dec 24	Got Xmas tree ready and Mrs Taylor and family goes Devonport for Xmas.
Dec 30	A Snell and I went Smeaton after church and heard preaching on wireless 1st time.

CHAPTER EIGHTEEN

Cherry Ripe

by Natalie Allen

I spent my childhood at Birchenhayes Farm, situated in a deeply wooded valley between St Mellion and Halton Quay. Old maps indicate that there was a house on the site, as long ago as 1680, but I am of the opinion that the earliest homestead was the semi-ruined, thatched building which was still standing in the orchard, some distance away from our farmhouse, during the time we lived there. The property was part of the Pentillie Estate.

One Richard Parken lived at Birchenhayes in 1841 and in March 1871, William Parken took over the tenancy on a fourteen year lease, at a rental of £60 per annum. In 1879 William's daughter, Jane, married James Dymond Langsford, the third child of Charles Langsford of Radland Mill, and they also lived at Birchenhayes.

They had a daughter in 1880, but she died when she was three years old. Five years later, James's wife died, aged 35. James was devastated at the loss of his wife and child, but two years later he married his late wife's sister, Mary Emily. In 1890 their first child, Ethel was born. James Dymond Langsford had three other daughters and two sons. His eldest son, Reginald, born 17th March 1894, was my father.

In 1905, James took over the tenancy of the farm from his father-in-law and he farmed there until his death in 1924, aged 74. When James first married in 1879, six acres of adjoining land known as Brentswood was described as an oak coppice. Over the next few years, this area was ripped by James and his father-in-law and when the south-facing land was cleared, it was planted up with wild cherry saplings which, when rooted, were grafted by James. It is not known from where these original grafts were obtained, but the first fruiting trees produced in Brentswood were named 'Birchenhayes Early' and these cherries were very juicy and sweet. Another variety was named after the nearby farm, Burcombe, where the Parken family lived at one period. This type bore larger fruit and later proved to be very suitable for bottling, for use in the winter months. Yet another variety was named 'Upright', which was really a descriptive name, as the branches of the trees grew in an upward form, unlike the drooping branches of the other types. However, I have not been able to discover why the variety 'Bullion' was so named – perhaps Grandfather hoped it would be a money-spinner!

Many years elapsed before the trees produced sufficient fruit to be profitable, but by the 1930s they had reached full fruitfulness and were massive trees, some forty feet high.

Cherry picking was not for the faint hearted. It was not easy to climb a forty bar ladder in a stiff breeze and keep ones balance merely by leaning against the ladder. It was impossible to hold on to the ladder, because cherry picking was a two-handed job. It meant reaching out to capture a branch with one hand and then, with a slight backward tug, the fruit was pulled off the twig by its stalk. This was not a job for a heavy handed person, as the fruit had to be handled with care, for if the berry was pulled from it's stalk or squashed, it would rot within a few hours. No doubt that is why many women made good pickers, as they treated the fruit gently.

My mother loved picking cherries and would work alongside the men folk all day, only asking for assistance when the long, cumbersome ladders needed to be moved to a new position in the tree. Locals referred to each position as a 'coose'.

Usually a tree could be picked in half a dozen moves, as experienced pickers would stretch to reach fruit from a wide area. Each worker had his, or her, own strong cane bucket shaped basket with a cane handle, but it also had a detachable S-shaped metal hook, which enabled the basket to be hooked securely over a bar of the ladder, thus leaving both hands free to pick fruit. Even the most nimble fingered, found it difficult to fill their basket in less than an hour and it held about

Brentswood Now ...

... and Then

This sepia photograph shows
Brentswood in its heyday,
viewed from Tremoan Hill.
c.1940.

The interior of Bill Cook's
packing shed. This is the only
remaining shed in what was
once a busy market garden,
Brentswood. Breakfast, crib
(snack) and dinner was
prepared and eaten in sheds
of this type. Note the
open hearth. c.1996.

George and Freda Brown's stone packing shed stands as a memorial to all the market gardeners who once worked in Cotehele Valley. *c.*1999.

Gateway to Comfort Wood. *c.*1999.

The Jam House at Haye. *c.*1999.

twelve pounds of fruit. The cherries were tipped from the picking baskets into chips that were spread under the trees in the shade. At the end of each session, the chip baskets were taken to the packing shed to be sorted and weighed. The fruit picked by professionals needed little attention, but a newcomer to the job gave the sorters more work, as there were often under-ripe or rotten fruit and sometimes leaves and twigs, in their baskets.

If the fruit was to be sent long distances by rail, each chip would have a cardboard cover tied on, to protect the fruit, but even with only this light covering, there was rarely any pilfering in those days. The majority of our cherries were sold at the door or taken to shops in Looe, Liskeard or Saltash. Our regular customers at Saltash were Goodmans, 'Fruity' Freeman's and Mrs Jasper's. We never had any difficulty selling cherries, as they were very popular and not grown in many areas outside the Tamar Valley. Customers came from as far as Upton Cross and Egloskerry, to collect their annual cherry order.

I always accompanied Dad on the early morning trips to the shops. I helped to carry the chips into the shops, wrote invoices and collected the money. I enjoyed these outings and was glad that cherry time coincided with school holidays, which meant I was free to help out every day. I recall that when we reached the top of Fore Street in Callington there was usually a policeman on point duty there, as this was before the traffic lights were fixed. Dad used to lean out of the car window and give the policeman a handful of cherries much to his delight. He would then continue to direct the traffic, whilst discreetly spitting out cherry pips!

Lena Bennett and Flo Downing picking cherries at Brentswood. *c.1920s.*

I remember delivering fruit to an elderly lady named Mrs Currah who lived in West Looe and her talkative parrot always greeted me. Most of the shopkeepers were very friendly, but one shopkeeper at Liskeard always complained about the asking price and would poke the fruit about with his finger and if there should be one poor cherry in the chip, he would always find it! He would pick it up and dangle it in front of Dad's face, to prove his point concerning the quality of the produce on offer. On one such occasion Dad, a normally placid man, lost his patience and grabbed up the offending chip of cherries and walked out of the shop, leaving poor Mr Penfound without any cherries to sell that day! We also sold fruit to the Rich family at the corner shop at Addington and to Miss Rickard on the Parade and dear old Miss Crawford on Bay Tree Hill.

The weather was of great importance at cherry time, as a long period of rain meant that ripe fruit would split and go mildew on the trees. Starlings were also a menace. A flock of birds could clear a tree of fruit over night and they saw no fear. Dad would fire his shotgun into the air and the birds would fly off for a few minutes, only to return again in seemingly larger numbers. But in good weather, cherry time was wonderful. Many workers were employed on a temporary basis and could be heard shouting to each other or whistling cheerily, as they went about their work.

One man who worked for Dad regularly for some years during cherry time, was Jack Fursman Jnr. During the early part of the war he lodged with his (and my) Uncle Len Wilton at Rill. When I spoke to him a few years prior to his death, he recalled one lovely summer evening in particular, when the whole valley was filled with the sound of men singing. Apparently, one man on Albert Reep's ground at Halton Wood near Pill Head Bridge began to sing and he was joined by pickers nearby. Soon various workers took up the song all the way up through Brentswood and they sang together, like a choir. This incident is typical of the camaraderie that was always evident among the men and women who worked in the valley. Jack also told me of the time he and my father spent almost three days picking one particular 'Birchenhayes' tree. They gathered twelve chips of fruit from the ground without the aid of ladders and overall the tree produced 51 dozen-pound chips. Cherries were always sold by the 'dozen' which was the contents of one chip, twelve pounds. The fruit sold at that period for about £1 per dozen and Jack said he was paid 3/- (about 15p) a dozen. Cherry picking was considered to be a good job as a man could earn up to £2 a day if he was competent and prepared to work long hours. At that time a farm worker's wage was about £4 for a five and a half-day week.

Jack reckoned he picked one and a half tons of cherries in one good season at Birchenhayes and one Whitsuntide he picked one and a half hundred weight of gooseberries over the weekend, and they were sold at 5½d a pound, about two new pence in today's currency.

Of course, cherry time brought the annual influx of relations and friends whom we scarcely knew existed during the rest of the year! Just as seaside dwellers are visited in the summer by their friends and relations who 'just happened to be passing ', so we were invaded when the cherry season was in full swing. Aunts, uncles and cousins, were joined by current girl and boy-friends and in-laws and they all came on their annual pilgrimage to gather fruit to fill their larders for the coming winter. At times the traffic was so hectic, we felt we ought to install 'stop and go' lights, to prevent a collision in the narrow lanes!

I was always delighted to see these people, but it must have meant a lot of extra work for Mum, as after eating their fill of fresh cherries, they were invited indoors for cups of tea and cherry pie and cream. I have seen our large dining-room table full of people all chattering away, as this was often the only time they met up and all the news had to be exchanged.

Cherry pie was made with whole cherries including the stones, which were then discreetly spat into ones spoon and placed on the side of the desert plate. When we had eaten our fill of the luscious berries and cream the ritual of counting the stones had to take place. We children had to decide our fate by reciting the rhyme, 'Tinker, tailor, soldier, sailor, rich man, poor man, beggar man, thief', thus discovering the profession of our future husband! We had a fifty-fifty chance of marrying a man of some respectability, but as in all games of chance we were sometimes disappointed with the result. We then had to fain hunger in order to have a second helping of pie and thus, hopefully, obtain a more satisfactory partner when the stones were finally totalled up. We then had to discover when we were likely to meet this person, 'this year, next year, sometime, never', we chanted. To decide our wedding attire we sang 'silk, satin, muslin, rags', and 'coach, carriage, wheelbarrow, pram' for our mode of transport. Cherry feasts were much more exciting then dull apple or gooseberry tarts, and the same rigmarole took place every year without fail. As a grandmother I find myself surreptitiously reciting the verse on the rare occasions that I am able to obtain some cherries worthy of being made into a pie.

Dad's brother, Uncle Charlie, used to come from Bere Alston and stay at our house for a week or so at the peak of the season, and help pick fruit for market. I used to think this was very exciting, as we rarely had overnight visitors. I enjoyed listening to the conversations about Uncle's business associates and he brought a new dimension into my narrow life.

But visitors occasionally meant trouble and one incident in particular comes to mind. Our back-yard was shut off from the farmyard by a gate, which was religiously closed after use, to keep stray

The attractive label featured on tins of fruit canned at St Dominick. c.1930s.

Cherry blossom at Birchenhayes. c.1996.

Langsford's barge 'Dorothy', from a painting by Ryder of Plymouth.

De Caen anemones blooming in Francis Steer's garden. *c*.1961.

'Fortune' ready for packing.

Mary Martin, granddaughter of Harold Langsford, with partner James Evans, sampling the cider from the newly restored press at Westcott Farm near Callington. *c*.1980.

Mary, an accomplished artist, has captured the spirit of the Tamar Valley in her paintings of fruit and flowers. These are exhibited both locally and further afield. James, an engineer and railway preservation enthusiast has worked with Mary to recreate some of the valleys past glory. Together they have researched old varieties of apples and cherries, grafted new stock and planted a new but traditional orchard in the Cotehele Valley, thus ensuring the continuation of fruit growing in the Parish into the new century.

animals away from the back door. This rule was strictly adhered to during cherry time, as the chips of fruit were often stored here in the cool, on long forms, awaiting collection by various customers. On this particular evening, we all returned to the orchard after tea, as it was usual to pick until dusk. I could not climb the ladders, but I used to pick the fruit from the lowest branches and even my small contribution was a help when there was a glut of fruit, as cherries had to be harvested as soon as they were ripe, which often meant working long hours. The usual troop of friends turned up during the evening, and finding no one at the house, made their way to the orchards and joined us there. When we all returned, a terrible sight met our eyes. Someone had failed to close the gate properly and our old sow had entered the covered yard and completely ruined the whole afternoon's pick. The fruit was squashed and the baskets trampled underfoot. Juice ran down the path like deep purple blood and trickled into the gutter. We were all very upset, but nothing could be done except clear up the worst of the mess. There were a lot of disappointed customers that night.

By the early 50s, the trees were beginning to loose their vigour and produced smaller crops. This combined with the higher wages made the cost of picking the fruit prohibitive and the era of the black cherries of Brentswood was over. Sadly few trees now survive and my children have never tasted the luscious, juicy, black cherries, which used to grow so abundantly during my childhood. But the loss of the trees is two-fold, as it means the wonder of springtime blossom, has also gone forever.

If you can imagine the beauty of a tree laden with clusters of white blossom and multiply the vision five hundred fold, you will then have some idea of the magnificence of Brentswood in springtime. Nowhere in the world could you find a more breath-taking scene than the drifts of snow-white blossom stretching as far as the eye could see.

The branches met overhead like the graceful arches of a giant cathedral … the only sound was the drone of bees, as they lazily moved from flower to flower. A breeze which sent a gentle sigh through the valley, stirred the blossoms and soft white confetti drifted slowly down to the ground …

Bohetherick group c.1921.

Left to right: Fruit salesman, Harry Martin, Vera Medlin, Clara Martin and baby, Kathleen Wakeham, Nesta Gorman, Beat Cole, Sam Medlin, Ronald Martin, Cyril Striplin, Len Hughes, Joe Rickard, Wilfred Martin, Rhoda Striplin and Alfie, Lizzie Roberts, Nell Gorman, Garfield Rickard (sailor), Mary Rickard, Ben Rickard. *Seated*: George Rickard.

CHAPTER NINETEEN

King Alfred and the Spurs

by Natalie Allen

On the death of James Dymond Langsford in 1924, his son Reginald married Laura Martin of Jubilee Cottages and took on the tenancy of Birchenhayes Farm. In 1928 their daughter, Pamela was born and I was born five years later.

My own earliest memory, is of lying in my pram outside my parent's packing shed and hearing the chatter of workers as they bunched daffodils during the spring of 1935, when I was two years old.

When in the 1880s, Grandfather Langsford and a group of men of his generation, had pioneered the market garden industry in Brentswood and the adjoining Halton Wood, the six acres nearest Birchenhayes, was let with the farm. The remainder of the land was rented from the Pentillie Estate by different families, amongst them my maternal grandparents, John and Edith Martin of Jubilee Cottages. Each plot consisted of two or three acres and this was considered to be sufficient to provide a living for a family.

Most of the Langsford's ground was suitable for the use of horse-drawn implements, but those who rented land further down the valley, were on very steep ground, which had to be worked by

In this photograph (1914) the man and woman at the back are Edith Rebecca and John Henry Martin (Natalie Allen's maternal grandparents). Also in the back row is their eldest daughter Edie. Seated are their other two daughters Laura and Phyllis and the little child is Evelyn Morcombe. The young men either side are Ralph Carkeet and Jack Billing.

They are outside a packing shed on land at Brentswood worked by the Martin family of Jubilee Cottages until their retirement in 1936 when Jack Sambles took over the ground. The last person to cultivate this plot was Jack Talbot of St Mellion.

This shed was burnt down a number of years ago and the ground is now planted with conifers.

Bob Searle at work at Brentswood. *c.*1930.   Jack Smith working for Reg Langsford at Brentswood. *c.*1930.

hand. In later years, after the arrival of the motorcar, old trucks were stripped of their bodywork and used to winch ploughs and earth-moving scoops, from the bottom track, to the tops of the gardens, thus lessening the workload a little.

The cherry trees planted and grafted by Farmer Jim, as my grandfather was known, were flourishing in the 1930s and had been underplanted with thousands of daffodils and narcissi bulbs of different varieties. Some of the older types remained in the same piece of ground for years and always flowered prolifically. However, new varieties were introduced by the Dutch Salesmen who came across from Holland each year selling bulbs and anemone corms. Our earliest yellow daffodils were aptly named 'The First' and usually came into bloom soon after my birthday in early February, but the season got into full swing during March and April. During my early childhood, there were always plenty of helpers available and their chatter filled the air, as they skillfully bunched the blooms and counted the bunches into pails of water, only to have the benches immediately filled again by the men folk who were out picking in all weathers. It is easy to remember only the sunny days, when a gentle breeze stirred the dancing daffodils, but not every day was as idyllic as Wordsworth would have us believe. It was not pleasant to spend the day draped in old sacks, wellington boots and sou'wester battling against gales and rain, with sap oozing from each stem and soaking your clothes. Prior to the last war our full-time workman was Dick Peters and he and his wife Dorothy, Ambrose Whale, Jack Smith and Donald Jane all helped pick flowers for us at Brentswood. My sister, Pam, loved outdoor work and spent hours picking flowers and when she grew-up; much of her time was spent working on the land. She would tackle any job, including

Bob Searle, Alf Rickard, Carlos Cook, Win Olver, Roy Rickard (son of Alf), Bill Cook outside what was later Westlake Rickard's shed at Brentswood. Roy Rickard later took over the adjoining land from his father. c.1930.

harvesting, potato picking and milking. She always tended the poultry and as children we always had a pet cockerel as a playmate!

When war broke out and helpers were called to more important work, help became scarce. By this time, we had evacuees from Nottingham sharing our home. Margaret, Maureen and Dorothy Lewitt and their granny, Mrs Meakin, lived with us for about three years. Margaret made her home with us after the war was over and she became a secretary to Harry Thorpe who was a cabinet-maker in Callington. She later married Courtney Vanstone and worked with him on their market garden until her death. Our evacuees joined forces with Pam and I and we spent all our Easter holidays and evenings, helping with the flower harvest. We four older girls were of a similar age, between six and eleven years old, when the war started, but we soon learned how to pick daffodils properly. We could identify all the different varieties that Dad grew. I was delegated the job of writing the description of the contents onto the cover of each cardboard box as Dad packed them. The boxes were tied together in pairs and labelled ready to send to wholesalers at Covent Garden in London. We also sent produce to Leeds, Bradford, Manchester and Glasgow and to Smithfield Market in Birmingham. In early years, wooden boxes were used and I recall that we had a shed full

Ben Pengelly, Ned Cole, Bob Searle working for John Henry Martin at Brentswood. c.1930.

of boxwood sections, which Dad used to make up into flower boxes in the winter months, ready for the coming season.

In the early 1930s scores of boxes were trundled on a large, flat wheelbarrow, down a rough track at least half a mile long. Our land was furthest away from the road which meant our barrows being wheeled past the other gardens in Brentswood, before reaching Pill Head bridge, which was the pick-up point for the haulier.

The two acres next to us had been ripped by Richard Striplin in the 1880s and was worked by him for many years. I can just recall Maurice Rickard having the land and then Harry Rickard took over. This ground was steep and Harry constructed steps made from lengths of wood, which were fixed securely at each end with wooden pegs. These steps led right to the top of his garden and made access much easier, especially when carrying chips of fruit or peck baskets full of daffodils. Harry's ground was always immaculate and he was the last of the tenants to vacate the land, when the era of market gardening drew to a close. My sister was able to tell me, that he retired in September 1973. Pam has a very good memory for dates and I have asked her for information on numerous occasions, whilst compiling this book!

Evelyn Morcombe (Kitt) at Brentswood. c.1934.

Dick and Dorothy Peters and Ken, Ambrose Whale, Mrs E Cradick, Mrs Edith Downing and Michael Downing at Brentswood. c.1934.

Jack Smith and Dick Peters at Brentswood. c.1932.

Next to Harry was Bill Cook. His brothers, Carlos and Arthur also worked this land at some stage. Bill's packing shed was the last to succumb, when Brentswood ceased to be cultivated and I was able to photograph it, to include in this book (*see* page 112). It was typical of the packing houses which every grower owned. Jack Sambles, whose story was related in 'A Stitch in Time', worked the next few acres. My maternal grandparents Edith and John Henry Martin who lived at Jubilee from 1898 till 1936 previously worked this ground. Their cottage was taken over by Mr Sambles and Grandma and Grandad spent their last few years in Montrose House, (now renamed Penlee) in Vogus Lane. The photograph at the start of the chapter shows the Martins outside their packing house, where Grandma spent hours bunching flowers etc. and preparing the family's meals over the open fire which was built into the gable end of the shed. Most of the packing sheds had cooking facilities of some description, often an oil fired metal stove on which a kettle could be boiled. The other mod-con consisted of a wooden shack perched precariously over the stream, which ran along the bottom of each plot of land; on it's way to the River Tamar. This 'flushed' toilet was probably more hygienic than the earth closets, which many homes had well into the 1930s. Our packing shed had no cooking aids and the only toilet was about a quarter of a mile away in one of the orchards, and that was an earth closet and full of spiders and other creatures.

Westlake Rickard and his son Alan at Brentswood. c.1938.

Alan Rickard and Dad's Austin 7 at Pillhead Bridge. c.1938.

That reminds me of another incident! When I was about eleven, my private school at Callington closed and I was sent to St Hilary School in Saltash. At one time, inspired no doubt, by the adventures of some Enid Blyton character, I decided I wanted a few of my school friends to come to the farm and set up a camp. My mum was *not* enthusiastic about this, infact she refused point blank to even consider the idea, and I was none too pleased. The fact that we had no tent or indeed anything that remotely resembled one did not occur to me and I was determined to have my camp in the orchard. I played my final card. "There's a lavatory down there Mum, and even a big toilet roll". Surely this would win her over; but to my dismay she informed me that 'the big toilet roll', was a roll of tarred paper, used by Dad to tape around the apple trees at the appropriate time of year, to deter coddling moth! Needless to say my camping expedition failed to materialise.

But I must put that disappointment behind me, and tell you a little more about the tenants of Brentswood as I remember them in the 1940s.

Next to Jack Sambles was Westlake's ground. William Westlake Rickard was a bit of a character and was always fond of teasing anyone who would rise to his bait! He was one of a large family of children and he and his wife worked very hard on their few acres, as did all

Beatrice Rickard and Peter, Annie Holwill (*née* Sleeman), Hilda Sleeman and Alan Rickard. *c*.1941.

the tenants of Brentswood. As a family, we rarely travelled very far from home, but if we did venture to Viverdon or some such place for a drive, we always seemed to meet up with Westlake! When Dad drove us to see the new television mast on Hessary Tor, we thought we had gone to a foreign land, but who should we see when we parked our Austin 12 car? Why, Westlake Bill, of course! Even when we girls grew up and started to do a bit of courting, we were always spotted by Westlake, and teased unmercifully by him, when we next met!

Roy and Marjorie Rickard worked the last piece of ground in Brentswood and their land finished at the gateway which led on to Pill Head bridge. The gardens beyond that point were called Halton Wood. At Pill Head, Fred Rogers, a local haulier, would collect all the produce and take it to Saltash railway station. I also recall a chap called Reynolds, he always wore a leather apron and he used to drive a lorry, which ran to the Southern railway station. After a while, the gardeners at the end of the track, widened out the pathway, thus enabling lorries to come up as far as Bill Cook's packing shed, where a narrow turning area was constructed, so for a time we did not have to cart our goods so far. As years went by, a change of plan by the firm meant lorry drivers no longer visited each group of growers in the valley and produce had to be taken to more accessible points for collection. We were then obliged to load dozens of boxes into our Austin 12 saloon and drive a mile to the nearest pick-up point, which was Post Box on the main road to St Dominick. The boxes were loaded on to the drop down boot of our car and all the seating areas were filled. Boxes were piled precariously on the wings and tied to the front lights. The driver was compelled to drive with little or no visibility and could only hope and pray, he would not have the misfortune to meet P.C. Berryman on his bike, and be booked for driving a dangerous load!

Horace Barker and his son Sidney, picking strawberries at Crocadon Wood. Sid ripped this scrubland and cultivated it for some years during the 1940s. Horace Barker worked for Mr Reg. Langsford at Birchenhayes Farm until 1954.

The flowers were never sent to market until they were in full bloom and what a wonderful sight that was. An expertly packed box of 'Emperors' or 'Spurs', surrounded by tissue paper and held in place by a wooden stem-stick was a joy to behold. If any daffodils were picked in bud they would be kept overnight in a warm room to force them into bloom, before being bunched and prepared for market. Often our bath was commandeered to hold the flowers when every available bucket was in use, and the scent was sometimes quite over powering. Now wholesalers, quite rightly, I suppose, insist the flowers arrive at market in tight bud, with the head of the flower barely showing colour, gooseneck stage this was called in the old days. Of course the blooms last longer, but they never reach their full potential when not allowed to open naturally. A box of daffodils today is a sorry sight and I am surprised they sell as well as they do – they are not the cheery sight which heralded spring in my father's day.

We were never bored when bunching, as there were so many different types of daffodils. If we grew tired of bunching the long stemmed 'Brilliancy', we would spend a while doing the dainty little 'White Queens' or the majestic 'King Alfred' and we used to listen to the wireless if we were bunching at home in the evenings. We especially enjoyed being entertained by Robb Wilton with his tale of 'The day war broke out ...'

We always used rubber bands to secure our bunches of flowers and over a period of weeks, the skin around our nails would become very sore, by the continual pressure of stretching the rings to fit over the stems. Some people became allergic to either the sap or the pollen from daffodils, and were unable to work with the flowers in any capacity.

At one period Dad bought a wooden frame, which was supposed to help bunchers to produce a better-shaped bunch more quickly. We soon abandoned that bit of equipment when we found we could all do a better and quicker job the old way.

1941 was the worse period of the war for us and a great deal of the evening bunching was done in the air-raid shelter, as enemy planes droned overhead. Although our farm was very isolated, we were not far from Plymouth and the Dockyard, as the crow flies, so many a stray bomb landed in the vicinity. Dad, being of a nervous disposition, slept for weeks in the shelter and I, out of a mixture of fear and affection spent many a night there with him. Mum, meanwhile, in her own words 'preferred to die in her own bed'. But luckily, nothing too bad occurred although our workman, Mr. Barker, was dive-bombed one day whilst working the horses in our fields. The poor man returned to the farmyard complete with horses, at a rate exceeded at no other time during his employment with us!

During wartime it was difficult to obtain new cardboard boxes and the wholesalers used to return the used boxes by rail, to enable growers to re-use them time and time again. At one period we were reduced to using waxed cardboard boxes that had contained meat for the American soldiers, who were stationed in England. The stench when these boxes were opened was horrendous and it was not unusual to discover a slice of rotting beef adhered to the box. But the daffodils still sold well during the war years, despite the poor presentation. One grower in the village was noted for saying, 'We didn't *make* money during the war, we raked it in!' Although the produce sold well, I do not think many growers became millionaires!

OLD VARIETIES OF DAFFODIL

These old varieties of daffodil were grown by the Langsford family on the six acres of Brentswood which were part of the Birchenhayes Farm until the mid-1950s.

Many other 'up-market' varieties were produced by other neighbouring market gardeners.

The bulbs remained in the same ground from season-to-season and were not dug up, sterilised or replanted each year as the modern bulbs are today.

Many still survive amongst the grass and brambles of Brentswood and flower regularly – some 45 years later.

ACTEA
BARRI
BRILLIANCY
CREOSUS
EMPEROR
GOLDEN SPUR
HOSPODAR
KING ALFRED
JOHN EVELYN
LUCIFER
PEARL
ORNATUS
SCILLY WHITE
WHITE LADY
WHITEWELL
SUN RISE
THE FIRST
PRINCEP

BRIGHTLING
BATH FLAME
BONFIRE
CHEERFULNESS
EMPRESS
HELIOS
HORACE
KING GEORGE
LADY DIANA MANNERS
NIP
PHEASANT EYE
RED BEACON
DOUBLE WHITE
WHITE QUEEN
SIR WATKIN
WILL SCARLET
VICTORIA

My sister, Pamela Land
(*née* Langsford) c.1950s

CHAPTER TWENTY

Harvest Time

by **Natalie Allen**

Soon after the cherry season ended, we had to begin the task of harvesting our three fields of corn. We grew either black oats, barley, wheat or dredgecorn, which was a mixture of different grains. Before my time our corn was cut with a horse drawn binder, but by the late 1930s, tractors had taken over. Dad's nephew, Stuart Martin from Towell, was the first to cut our few acres by tractor.

In 1943 Jack Fursman junior invested £175 in a new tractor and began to undertake various tasks on farms around the village. Dad employed him to do ploughing and to cut our corn, and his charge in those days, was £1 per acre. He worked up quite a business over the years and in 1948, Jack purchased his second tractor, a Fordson Major, for £280. This one sported rubber tyres and lights, which was a vast improvement on the earlier model. Mr Buckingham, the saddler in Callington, usually did repairs to the binder canvasses when necessary.

Harvesting in those days was a slow, laborious task, but the atmosphere in the cornfields was much friendlier and satisfying than today. Now the corn is cut, threshed and put into store in one operation and the weather conditions are no longer so critical, as the whole procedure can be completed in a few hours. When the old methods were practised, weeks could elapse between the cutting and the actual harvesting, of the corn. Man became more involved in the battle against the elements and consequently felt more reason to rejoice when the harvest was finally gathered in.

Horace Barker and *Prince* at Birchenhayes Farm. *c.*1953.

In the pre-combine harvester days, as the binder cut and bound the sheaves, it would drop the sheaves at intervals over the field. We would all help to gather them together into the traditional stooks. This was done by erecting half a dozen sheaves in such a way, as to resemble a wigwam, with the heads of corn clustered together at the top and the base splayed out to prevent the sheaves falling over. Similar stooks were made every few yards in straight rows all around the field. When the 'fore-round' or outside round was completed, another row would be started further into the middle of the field, leaving sufficient distance between the rows for a horse and wagon to be driven along.

In ideal conditions, the corn would dry naturally within a few days and be ready to store in a large rick in the corner of the field, to await the threshers.

But the weather was not always kind and sometimes the stooks were in the fields for weeks, due to adverse conditions. If the sheaves were continually wet for any length of time, the grains of corn would begin to sprout and would then be useless. I can remember this happening at Birchenhayes, more than once. When the sun did see fit to shine for a few hours, we dismantled the stooks, loosened the wet sheaves and spread them around in an attempt to dry them out quickly, between the showers, in the hope of saving at least some of the crop.

But usually the sun shone and I can remember running through the newly cut fields, with the sharp stubble scratching my bare legs and stabbing my toes.

The day the corn was eventually ready to carry was the most exciting part of the harvest scene, when we were young. On that day, we made sure we were in the farmyard in good time to hitch a lift to the field on the horse-drawn wagon. We would sit on the hard wooden floor and hold tight to the sides of the wagon. I recall the crunching sound the wagon wheels made, as we trundled up the rough track to the cornfield. The vibration made it difficult to speak properly and we laughed with delight to hear our voices, which sounded gruff and unfamiliar. Once inside the field the ride became less bumpy. As the soft turf cushioned the wheels, the harsh sound receded to a smooth whirring noise and the long grass muffled the clatter of the horse's hoofs and our childish voices were once more under control.

At harvest time, Mum would make vast quantities of lemonade. She dissolved Eiffel Tower lemonade crystals in sweetened boiling water and when cooled and suitably diluted, this produced a refreshing drink. We children saved the small screw topped bottles, which had held the yellow crystals and filled them with lemonade, to take to the fields with us. We put them in a convenient rabbit-hole to keep cool. We then selected a length of golden straw to suck our lemonade through. Our straws were much stronger than those bought from a shop and had a special flavour, which became associated with harvest time. We held a contest to see who could keep their straw intact for the longest period.

On the back and front of the wagon, lathes were fixed to hold the load in place. Two large coils of rope were suspended from the back lathes and were used to secure the load if it was to be taken a long distance. The ropes were not in use during the loading of the wagon and we used to jump up and straddle the loops of rope and swing on them as the wagon trundled along. The sticky isles of the barley and bits of straw would drift down from the load and get into our hair and inside our clothes.

One man rode on the wagon and made the load, balancing precariously, as the load grew higher and higher. Two or three others pitched the sheaves from either side of the wagon and the stooks gradually disappeared as the wagon was slowly pulled between the rows. Sometimes, my sister would guide our Shire horse, taking care to keep her feet well away from Prince's large hoofs. The smell of leather harness and horse sweat mingled with the scent of the fresh straw, and became part of the sensual aroma that was harvest. Often the horse was left to his own devices and a short command to "Get on," or "Whoa", was all that was needed to control his movements. But occasionally, Prince would ignore the call to stop and would continue to plod along at his usual steady pace, leaving the men with a sheaf on the end of their pikes and no wagon on which to toss it. The normal peacefulness of the picturesque scene would be shattered as the men bawled out, "Whoa, damn you. Whoaaa!" After a moment's hesitation, Prince would decide that three against one, was hardly fair play and would give in graciously, to their demands and revert to the stop-go routine that he had previously followed.

When the wagon was stacked as high as was practicable, the load would be taken across the field or to the mow-hay and added to the steadily growing rick. At the end of the day the rick was covered with a tarpaulin to keep it dry. When the rick was finally 'made-off', that is to say gradually built up to resemble the roof of a house, the whole thing would be covered with galvanised sheets and made safe for the winter. I cannot remember any of our ricks being thatched, in my time.

I recall hearing the distinctive call of the now virtually extinct, corncrake. Its call would carry quite some distance and resembled the sound of a creaking gate. I remember hearing them calling from the fields across the valley from our farm, at Tremoan. Our mother used to tell us that corncrakes were so numerous and noisy around the fields at Jubilee Cottages, when she was young, that everyone got annoyed by them. Cuckoos too were very plentiful each spring in those days, but are rarely heard in the village now.

Harvesting also gave us the added bonus of a picnic tea. Mum would come to the field with a large peck basket laden with jam sandwiches, scones and saffron cake. Hot tea was brought in an enamel ewer and despite the long journey, the tea always stayed piping hot. We all sat around on sheaves of corn and ate the feast, pausing now and then to remove the inevitable Kami Karzi insect that always seemed to fall into our teacups. At no other time did food ever taste so good.

I remember walking through the woods with Dad and the rest of the family, to see the first combine harvester at work at Crocadon Farm. Tommy Martin invited a number of local farmers to view the latest technology. Everyone was amazed to discover that this new machine could complete the harvesting of a field of grain, so quickly with the aid of only one man. In later years Dad employed Mr Crago from St Ive to do the harvesting on our farm and the age of the binder and the threshing machine was over. Gone too, was that wonderful atmosphere that had always prevailed at harvest time in the past.

Tosti, Roger, Gladys, Eliza and Edgar Langsford of Cleave Farm. c.1911.

1929

Jan 14	Went to hear Trenance lecture an mine sweeping.
Jan 24	I 'oakered' the house (??).
Feb 7	Planted 15 plum trees (1/- each), 2 Primate, 2 President, 1 Monark, 3 Bella Lavain, 4 Cox's Golden Drop and 3 Laxton's Early.
Feb 13	Mrs Worth a son.
Mar 2	Jack Taylor unwell and W Roberts drove 'One and All' and Leslie Babb and Mary Stephens married.
Mar 9	Leonard Cradick took Greenbank.
Mar 10	A Jope and I took trip to Greenbank.
Mar 23	Kathleen Sleep's husband died.
Mar 29	Phyllis and party came down to spend evening and we 'waid' M Snell 182 lb., J S 181 lb. Ern 146, Peg 40 lb.
Apr 21	Frost ice as thick as 3d piece and a lot of cherry blossom out and strawberry blossom badly cut.
Apr 14	A Plymouth man came to Taylor's and sold them a car.
May 31	Mrs Cox a daughter.
July 21	Charlie Cox's baby christened (Kit Jope's 1st).

Aug 8	Edgar Langsford married.
Aug 20	Went to Padstow, Port Isaac, Delabole, and Bodmin Prison for trip.
Oct 1	Fred Rogers goes Plymouth for operation and Mrs Lesley Babb a daughter.
Oct 5	Mrs Monty Rogers a daughter and Polly Sleeman died.
Nov 14	Northcott sent me bill for House Tax 12/6 for half year.
Nov 19	Nick Striplin burnt down his motor house and 2 cars etc. and W Friendship and his brother Jack ran into Co-op lorry with a motor bike.
Nov 20	W Friendship goes to hospital.
Nov 28	Tom Martin Brendon married.
Dec 5	Saltash ferry chain broke and ferry drifted up river.
Dec 8	Very stormy and Duke's engine house gives notice.
Dec 10	Went up Smeaton to help to right up the engine house.
Dec 17	A Snell went to Callington to do her Christmas shopping.

1931

Jan 13	I oiled the apple trees to keep away the rabbits and went to Victory hall to hear Dr Lawry lecture on Spain.
Jan 19	Little Dot Taylor poorly. (*Dr called everyday for 5 days, better service then today.*)
Feb 19	Insured car 3rd party £5 with Tom Pascoe.
Mar 31	Went Elbridge Motor hoe Show. (*Exhibition for Auto-culto*).
Apr 3	J Taylor went badger hunting.
May 10	Mrs W Taylor a son 2am.
May 29	J Taylor's new car arrived.
July 16	Bought auto cultivator.
Aug 15	Mr James Lawry died.
Sept 14	Auto culto misbehaving itself and J Taylor had a look at it. Mr Striplin finished Taylor garage.
Sept 16	Roberts came down to right auto culto 1/-.
Sept 29	W Roberts brought me down a plug for auto culto.
Oct 29	Phyllis netting (knitting) with 4 needles 1st time.
Nov 12	Old tin man called and took his basket of tins and gave us a Daily paper.
Nov 13	Biscombes brought galvanise and I made shelter for auto culto.
Nov 18	Attended lecture by ABBIS advising us what to grow as French vegetables are excluded due to Colorado beetle order.

1932

Mar 4	J Taylor ran over Chum the Bulldog.
Apr 20	J Taylor told me he was leaving Radland for Churchtown.
May 2	Finch came down for Taylor's waterwheel and fowl house.
May 17	Went Plymouth to sell 30 dozen cabbages to shops at 10d a dozen.
May 24	Market. Cabbage made 6d dozen, rhubarb 6d lb., Double whites 9d potatoes 7/- cwt.
June 28	Taylor's left Radland Mill.
June 30	Streams of rain after 3 weeks dry.
July 16	Old Mrs Jope died (Arnold's mother).
July 23	Raspberries made 10d for 2lb chip.
July 26	Took 54 chips raspberries to Co-op jam store over ripe. Poor sale.
Aug 3	Raspberries 7d and 8d 2 lb. chips. Potatoes 4/11 cwt, cabbage 1/3 dozen.
Sept 3	Went Corneal thrashing.
Nov 30	Met new neighbours 1st time, Mr Hambridge and son.
Dec 30	Quite a lot of new daffodil seedlings coming up.

1934

Jan 29	Went to Bodmin to the 'assises' (*assizes*) on the jury.
Mar 13	Alice Snell whitewashed the cow house.
Apr 4	Went Callington to see W Taylor beat a good little Liskeard boy on points.
Apr 11	Had a box with young W Taylor.
Apr 16	Sent £3.0.6d for licence for car.
May 30	Mrs Lewees Oliver (*Louise*) came down to see if we could sell her some wood.
Aug 1	Streams of rain after a long drought.
Sept 4	Went Kelly Bray with 22 chip figs for Ridley.
Sept 6	Ridley 18 chips figs.
Sept 10	Planted 1040 snowdrops.
Nov 23	Men putting phone wires up through coach drive.
Dec 8	Nelson Langsford's 2nd daughter married.
Dec 15	Parson Square died 10.30pm.
Dec 19	Went to Mr Square's funeral.
Dec 27	Christmas Glory out in bloom.

CHAPTER TWENTY-ONE

A Woman's Work

by Natalie Allen

Despite having the daily household tasks to cope with, practically every woman in the village worked alongside her husband on the land. The wives of market gardeners and farmers alike were always expected to share the outdoor work, especially during busy periods.

The daffodil season, closely followed by fruit picking stretched over many months, and when a whole family's livelihood revolved around a two or three acre plot of land, this often meant a wife working almost full-time throughout the year. The preparation of meals and general household duties including the laundry, was always the wife's domain. Coping with a home, a family and a career outside the home, is difficult enough today with all the electronic mod-cons now available. But sixty years ago few housewives had such labour saving devices. Every household task had to be performed by hand and even a change in wind direction, could mean the difference between a roaring stove and a sulky one, making it nigh-on impossible to guarantee the precise minute a meal would be ready to serve.

For the stove to function at all, it was necessary to sweep the flue pipes and the areas of the range that spread heat to the oven. This task had to be done weekly and in our home, Friday morning was usually set aside for cleaning the flues and black-leading the stove. It was a very dirty job; a brush was used for the smoke pipes and tools supplied with the stove were specially designed to scrape soot and ash from around the oven area. Mum always kept a goose-wing (retrieved when plucking the Christmas goose) and this made a handy, flexible 'brush' for getting into odd corners. This procedure inevitably created a lot of dust and dirt, so after the stove was cleaned the stone floor of the kitchen had to be scrubbed. We always had cocoa matting on the floor and during the week these were always protected with hessian covers. These were really just the large sacks that had held flour or corn. They were split open length-ways and the rough edges stitched around to make them presentable. Two such sets of hessian covers were made, so that dirty ones could be scrubbed each week. For some reason, best known to Mum, after the Friday clean-up the covers were not replaced and the 'best' mats were on view over the weekend. Come Monday morning, the covers were always in place again!

The crackling of faggot-wood heralded the start of washday. All the hot water for our laundry had to be boiled up in the furnace, which was situated alongside a cloam sink outside the kitchen door. The copper was filled with water and the starting wood was placed on the iron grid beneath the copper boiler and set alight. Providing the wood was dry and the wind in the right direction, there was every hope that the water would be ready for use in an hour or so. After the small twigs had 'caught-up', the fire was fed with large lengths of wood brought from the woodpile in the mow-hay across the farmyard. This wood was not sawn into logs like that used in our open fire indoors, but were quite often poles about six to eight feet in length. One end was placed in the fire and the remainder protruded onto the floor and was pushed into the flames as the ends burnt down. This took quite a few hours, and Mum spent most of washday avoiding them as she went about her work.

When boiled the water was transferred to the sink in buckets and the job of washing the clothes by hand, commenced. The copper was refilled and when the water was hot enough, an old sheet was placed inside to line the copper, because sometimes the same equipment was used to boil wheat to feed the pigs!

The 'whites' were hand washed, rinsed in cold water, then placed in the copper with a handful of Persil or washing soda and allowed to boil for half an hour to bring out the stains. I often helped out, by poking the clothes with a special stick to keep them under the boiling water, but as fast as I pushed one item down, another would billow up like a big balloon. The whole affair was rather hazardous, because if the fire burnt too fiercely, there was always the risk of the soapy water boiling out over. After the boiling session, the clothes were returned to the sink and rinsed with cold water until the water ran clear. This procedure was repeated until all the clothes were washed. The final rinse of the 'whites' was the most interesting, as a knob of 'Blue' was placed in a square of cloth and swished around in the water, turning it bright blue. I always feared the laundry would all be permanently dyed sky blue, but after being immersed for a few minutes, the items reappeared looking as white as those on today's television commercials!

Mum needed help to fold the largest sheets and tablecloths and these were then fed between the rollers of the iron mangle. When I grew big enough I helped by turning the handle which set the wooden rollers in motion. Soon all the water was squeezed out into a bucket and the clean clothes neatly deposited in tidy folds on a board behind the rollers.

Pillow cases, collars and aprons were always starched and this meant mixing a few spoonfuls of powered starch with a little cold water. Boiling water was then added and the articles were dipped into the mixture and then hung out to dry. Our clothesline was suspended between two apple trees in the back garden. After everything was firmly pegged on, the line was hoisted up as high as possible with the aid of a long pole with a forked top, which held the line. This prop was securely wedged into the ground and the clothes held aloft, well out of reach of the muddy grass below. On occasions, the prop would blow down or break and the whole wash would be found strewn around in the mud, and had to be rinsed and mangled again.

I liked the sunny, breezy days when the washing seemed to come to life and Dad's long-johns would cheekily entwine themselves with Mum's petticoat. All the socks would dance a special jig, as though delighted to be allowed to play in the sun. Seeing clothes pegged on a modern-day rotary dryer gives me a feeling of sadness. The items loose their identity and hang in a solid mass, with nothing to do and no freedom to go anywhere except round and round in monotonous circles, like prisoners exercising in a prison yard. Our clothes appeared to have little adventures and were free to frolic with the wind or to doze contentedly in the midsummer sun, and in the winter, they had the comfort of the kitchen range.

Ironing was done with a box iron. This was an iron-shaped container with a lift-up door at the back and was heated by inserting a block of metal which had previously been made red hot in the embers of the kitchen stove. Two slabs were needed, one being heated in the fire whilst the other was in use. As one cooled it was replaced by the hot one, which was handled with a long pair of tongs. It was rather tricky changing over the slabs and if all the ash was not removed, this would sometimes deposit itself on the clean clothing, leaving sooty marks.

In the1940s, Mum bought an iron that was heated by burning metholated spirits. I considered this one more hazardous than the old box iron, as it worked on the same principle as a primus stove and had to be warmed-up over a burner filled with spirits, which often flared up in a mass of blue flame. By the time we left the farm in 1954, we were using a Calor gas iron that proved to be very efficient and a Calor gas boiler replaced the old copper, which made washday a much simpler operation. But even at that period all the laundry work still had to be done in the same draughty alleyway.

No doubt, Mum was not the only woman in the village to work in such conditions. What a boon an automatic washing machine would have been to the hard working wives of yesterday.

1935

Feb 2	Little girl Tink married.		Aug 1	Mrs Rosekilly a daughter.
Feb 3	A Jope goes out to dine.		Sept 7	Florrie Taylor a new bike.
Feb 7	Duke and Brown's ferret laid up in Frank Rogers's hedge.		Sept 19	Finished taking up bulbs for sterilising and went to see Fred Rogers about it.
Feb 27	SouthWestern flower lorry runs 1st time this year.			
May 6	Jubilee sports. K Babb won show cycle race and Fry won fast cycle race. Miss Marion Fry won women's race.		Oct 2	Willis Rosekilly's car tipped over old Mr Striplin.
			Oct 26	Went to see Harvey fight.
May 17	Very sharp frost everything cut down, then a snowstorm.		Nov 28	Duke and Brown rabbitting caught 7.

CHAPTER TWENTY-TWO

Finding my next narrator was a bit like looking for a needle in a haystack!

I had been advised by several of my contacts that if I wanted another good tale I should pay a visit to Aubrey Gale 'down Baber'.

In my ignorance, I set off without getting more precise directions and my first stop was at Baber Farm, or at least what was Baber Farm in Fred Hancock's time, when I was a youngster.

This was my first mistake as the present owner of that property did not know of any Mr Gale. So I apologised for disturbing him and proceeded to call at four other homes in the vicinity where to my amazement I was given the same reply, 'Sorry I don't know anyone by that name'.

It was at this point that I realised just how much the character of the village had changed. It was no longer the close knit community I had once known. Then everyone knew each other and were on Christian name terms at least with their nearest neighbours. Now with the construction of new flats and houses many new families had moved into the area, but they do not work as farmers, market gardeners, tailors, cobblers or butchers in the village with daily contact with each other. Their business is conducted in the nearby towns or in Plymouth or further afield and their houses are often empty all day as they commute to their jobs. This leaves little time for bonding with neighbours or joining in with local activities. That combined with the fact that many of the older generation have now passed on and their children have moved away means the village has begun to move into the 21st Century and left me behind!

When I read reports in the weekly newspaper concerning happenings in St Dominick I hardly recognise a name. Gone are the Trenances, Northcotes, Grills and Finches. Dare I say even the Langsfords are now thin on the ground! What has become of all the 'Dominickans' I used to know?

But I have to admit at this stage, that even I didn't know Aubrey Gale! He had lived all his young life out 'Berry way' and lets face it that was too far for me to have ventured, way back in the 1940s, when I last resided in the Parish!

But at last my persistence was rewarded. I knocked on another door and there was Aubrey Gale.

He welcomed me warmly although I doubt if he knew anymore about me other then I was a 'Langsford maid'. But that was enough to set Aubrey's mind into top gear and soon we were chatting like old friends. Here I felt quite at home again as the conversation was splattered with references to the Langsford clan.

Cap'n was able to fill in a number of gaps left during previous consultations with villagers.

Although Aubrey was obviously keen to make his usual foray to his market garden at Fullaford where he still works every day, this sprightly 77 year old was happy to talk to me and I am delighted to include his story in my ever increasing store of village memoirs.

Cap'n Gale

by Aubrey Gale

I am Aubrey Gale and I have lived all my life in St Dominick. I was born in Berry Cottage 77 years ago. My father Hedley worked for Mr Arnold Jope at Higher Berry Farm and I spent my childhood in the farm worker's cottage. Mr Jope's parents had lived in a nearby cottage called Lower Berry, but Arnold Jope later built the larger farmhouse and moved there. He had seven children. Lower Berry was then converted into two adjoining cottages and various tenants lived there over the years. I lived in one for many years after I married. At that time Wilfred and Evelyn Kitt lived next door. The building that is now the home and studio of the artist Mary Martin, was a stable when I was a boy. If father was working the horses in the field up above our home and he hadn't finished off the job at the end of the day, he would stable his horse in that place instead of taking it up to Higher Berry Farm. Father would shout down over the hedge to me as I played in our garden and I would go to him and be put astride the great carthorse. My legs used to be stretched right out as I was only young and I would hold tight to the irons on the horse's harness and ride to the stable.

I married Ellen in 1941 and except for a few years after the war, when we lived in the mill house at Radland, we stayed at Lower Berry Cottage till the farm was sold.

The Cradicks bought our cottages at that time, but we stayed on and paid rent to Mrs Cradick until this council house in Baber Court became available. We moved here in June 1977.

Those two cottages have been converted back into one again now and Derek Cradick's daughter Janet lives there at present. The small cottage where I was born and the farmhouse have been sold off and Mr Poad owns the fields.

When I was a little lad I contracted tuberculosis and I did not go to school until I was six years old and then only half-days for sometime as I had to lead an outdoor life as much as possible with plenty of fresh air. Because I had time on my hands I used to visit Harold Langsford's corn mills as they were only a few yards down the lane from my home.

The workmen down there got to know me very well and that is how I got my nickname 'Cap'n'. Of course in the early days barges used to come to Cotehele Quay with grain to

Cap'n Gale. c.1999.

be crushed at the mills and the boss of the barge was Captain Martin from up Bohetherick. The bosses of the mines which once thrived in the Tamar Valley were always known as Mine Captains too. When I got to know Mr Langsford's workman Pikey Rich, he sort of took me under his wing and would take me with him in the cab of his lorry when he carted the grain around. When we went to a farm he would say to the farmer "I've got to behave myself today, I've got the 'Cap'n' with me", meaning me, and the name stuck. Everyone's called me 'Cap'n' since I was a small boy.

When the barges were still using the river, about twice a week, depending on the tides, Mr Langsford's two lorries would be driven to Cotehele Quay and Monty Rogers and Pikey Rich would unload the barge. One lorry load would be taken to the nearby Cotehele Mill, now owned by the National Trust, and the other would carry on to the bigger Glamorgan Mill opposite the lane leading to our home. The Cotehele Mill would take delivery of two loads to Glamorgan's one as it was built below the road and the large two hundred weight sacks of grain could easily be wheeled in through the doorway at road level right to the grinding area. At Glamorgan the lorry would be unloaded at ground level and all the sacks had to be hoisted up on pulleys to the top floor of the building. If no other help was available Mr Langsford used to send his children up to my mother to say "can 'Cap'n' come down and give a hand as soon as possible". My job was to hitch a rope securely around the neck of the sack, then give it a tug to say it was ready, then stand well back and Monty would hoist the sack up to the top. He'd then unhitch the rope and send it down to me and I'd repeat the procedure till all the sacks were moved. Mr Langsford would pay me 1/- for doing that job. It would take the best part of a day to unload a barge.

Bill Avery was a preacher from Harrowbarrow and he and Jack Coles worked at the mills in those days too.

At a later date when Mr Langsford's family moved to Bartletts, Charlie Sambles worked at the mill and he lived in the mill house below the road. George Langsford lived at Murden Farm and Jack Langsford and his family at Newhouse nearby.

I could drive the lorries before I was fourteen years old because Pikey Rich used to let me sit on his lap and steer the lorry when I was very young. As time went by, if it was safe for me to do so, Pikey would say "You turn the lorry round Cap'n". I would turn in the farmyard and have the lorry ready for him to drive back to the mill. I got to know how to work all the machinery in the mill and I could do any of the jobs. You could open up a shutter with a lever from inside the mill, pull it back to let the water from the leat into the wheel and the more water you let through the faster the wheel turned. You might have it running slow to crush oats, then faster to grind maize. I spent hours down at Mr Langsford's mill.

In the old days we boys would wander through all the fields and nobody ever bothered. We didn't do any damage and as long as we shut the gate behind us, we could go over anyone's land. Sometimes you might hear a voice say "You didn't shut that gate boy", you wouldn't even see the person but they knew you were about and you went back and closed the gate properly. We didn't climb hedges – always used the gates and treated the place with respect. That way we had freedom to travel miles. We'd roam from Dillets through the fields to Comfort 'ood and we'd catch trout in the stream out there. Tom Martin farmed at Brendon then and he'd see us and say, "Caught anything today then boys?" Nobody told us to go and we spent hours amusing ourselves like that.

We always went to the harvest fields too when they were saving hay. The farmers had to wait for a long dry spell so that the grass dried out well before being loaded on to carts and taken to the rick. We always got good food on those occasions because the farmer's wife would bring out baskets full of pork, beef and cake stuff.

"You've all been working hard, come and have something to eat", they would say and we would be invited to join the men though we hadn't really done anything!

Farmers helped each other at harvest time and Father would be up Tom Martins and their men would help out the Jopes. 'Twas always like that in those days. Sometimes, there would be a jar of cider and the men would say "Do 'ee want a sip Cap'n?" and we'd all have a drop of cider.

Mr Langsford made cider down Glamorgan. They had a cider house alongside the mill. Every farmer had an orchard at that time and if they didn't have their own cider press they would bring along their apples to the mill to be crushed. It took two or three days to make, depending on how much fruit each grower brought. The first day the apples were put through a chaff cutter and then put in layers with straw on the press. They would be pressed and left for a time to drain, then you tidied up the 'cheese' and pressed again. As soon as the first juice began to run the men would say "Where's Cap'n? Come on boy and tell us how it is" and I'd have the first drop to try. Then it was put into oak barrels and taken away and the whole place cleaned up ready for the next farmer's crop. They would come from everywhere and there was always someone there to help with the cider making.

I remember Edgar Langsford and Tucker Hunn's father George bringing apples there and a lot of Metherell farmers used Mr Langsford's cider press.

I went to school with Phyllis Duke and Florrie Taylor's sister. I remember the Taylors fixed up a small waterwheel in the stream below Dillets and it worked a generator. They had electric in their cottage at Radland Mill when we were still using oil lamps and candles.

Joe Snell grew marvellous flowers down Radland Mill gardens and he specialised in spirea. I've seen his packing house full of buckets of pink and white spirea waiting to be sent to market. Miss Alice Snell was a very reserved lady with little to say, but she always worked on the land hoeing and picking flowers and fruit. Each year when the Church flower service came around she always made up a huge bunch of mixed flowers for me to take to church as my contribution. The flowers were arranged symmetrically, with one large bloom in the middle and different types neatly placed in rings around it. I think she provided flowers for the other local children too. I recall visiting Joe and Alice every Sunday afternoon when I was a boy. I believe the two Luxton boys delivered Joe's copy of the Sunday paper at our house and I then took it down the lane to the Snell's house. Once Joe showed me how to make a wheel out of matchboxes and after that they always saved all their empty matchboxes and gave them to me to make models with. Joe always had time for us and was always friendly. He had a Ford lorry and drove it to Plymouth market.

Aydon Langsford's grandfather and Harold Langsford down Mill had the first two Morris Litre lorries in the Parish. They bought them from Callington Motors and both were ordered and painted up at the same time, but Langsford of Harrowbarrow registered his first. I believe the next one to have a lorry of that type was Cradick's down Greenbank but I'm not sure about that. Anyway when Aydon had their farm sale some while ago they still had that lorry complete with all the original documents and receipts for every gallon of petrol they had ever bought. I believe Callington Motors bought back that lorry and gave more for it then it had cost new, as it was the very first one they had sold all those years before.

Pikey Rich taught me how to drive in Harold Langsford's lorry, but I don't know where that one ended up.

During the war I was in the Royal Airforce for about four years. When I came home in 1945, Father took Radland mill house for Ellen and me. It belonged to Mrs Bessie Langsford then. A strip of land and the ruined barn across the stream belonged to Harold Langsford. I asked if I could rent the barn and re-roof it to keep a pig and some poultry. I can hear him now. "Have it Cap'n" he said "I don't want no rent off you". He was like that, always very good to me. We didn't stay at the mill long, as soon as Lower Berry Cottage became available in the late 1940s we moved up there.

The Jopes, Father and I all kept a pig for ourselves and when Father killed his, Mr Jope would help 'scrape' it and cut it up and Father would do the same for him. They both helped us the first time we had one to kill as I didn't know much about that job. They showed my wife how to rub the coarse salt into the joints of pork before putting them in a trundle. She was delighted. She came from up country and had never seen anything like that before. She wrote and told her family she had salted in a pig. She loved that job and never forgot the experience and often talked about it afterwards.

In 1948 I worked for Glover & Uglow as a driver, then they were taken over by English China Clay and they closed the Kelly Bray depot and I had to work in the Plymouth depot then. Work got a bit slack and they made a lot of men redundant. About that time, whilst I was still in work, my Uncle Ernie Gale died. He was a conductor on Western National Buses at one period and he also had some ground out Fullaford, out towards Callington way. When he died his Will stipulated that everything was left to his daughters but couldn't be sold during his wife's lifetime. That left them in a quandary as the girls couldn't work the land and Aunt Mabel was in her mid seventies, so she asked me if I would take over the work and keep the produce. So that's what I agreed to do. I still work that ground now. I've got six tunnels there and grow tomatoes, cucumbers, peppers, courgettes and aubergines. I've got a few strawberries and autumn fruiting raspberries outside, but I get Horace Bunkum to plough the spare ground and just work in the tunnels. I don't like it at home all day; I like to keep busy in my garden. I like the wildlife and I've got bird boxes out there, but there aren't many birds around these days. When I started off out there, we had birds everywhere, flying in and out of the packing shed even when customers were there buying my produce. I think we lost a lot during that very hot summer in the mid-1970s and the numbers have never made up. I used to sell a lot of strawberries and potatoes at the gate and I still sell stuff now. When Mr Langsford sold Glamorgan Mill, the new owner started to turn it into living accommodation and he used to buy a lot of vegetables off me. We would get talking and I'd tell him a bit about the history of the place and he said, "You know all about the mills – You should write a book".

Joey Pridham from Harrowbarrow used to visit the pub there and one time some newcomers were there saying how pleased they were to have been able to buy fresh fruit and vegetables from a Mr Gale. Joey said, "oh you'm talking about Cap'n 'ent you?" Next time they called at my garden they said "We didn't realise you were a ship's captain" So I had to put them right about that, but all my old mates knew me by that name.

I used to play football and cricket with the Harrowbarrow teams. A few weeks ago I was looking at an old photograph of the team. There were twenty men including the reserves, but only two or three of us are left now.

I still drive myself to work everyday. I keep pretty well and look after myself since my wife died. I always have a hot meal every evening, always have done. Sunday's I have a roast dinner at my daughter's place. But sometimes if I want to relax I go out and have a meal. You can get a good meal out cheaper than you can cook it at home these days.

You'm lucky to catch me in this morning as I was just off to work. John Friendship has been up to have a chat today – he always calls in on Tuesdays, Thursdays, Saturday and Sunday. On the other days he gets collected by car and taken to Chyvarhas Day Centre in Callington for the day. He loves that, they treat him well in there and he gets a good meal and plenty of company.

I'm always glad to see John arrive for a chat about the old days and to put the world to rights!

But every thing's changed now and the village isn't like it was when we were boys together. There's a different atmosphere altogether. Many of my old mates are gone, but I still remember them and the good times we had together.

John Friendship, Tommy Earl, Florence Friendship, Mary Martin, Mrs Seymour, Eric Earl, Ronald Martin, Jack Loam. The tub was used to send raspberries to the jam factory. c.1930s.

1936

Jan 11	Insurance stamps raised to 1/8d.
Jan 20	King died.
Feb 11	A S plastered up rat's holes in dairy.
Feb 28	For market 2 dozen eggs, 14 bunches daffodils, 6 violets, 6 primroses. Dafs made 2d primroses 1d bunch.
Mar 7	Went Comfort Wood. Elyoos (*Helios Daffodils*) showing colour in Symond's ground.
Mar 14	F & F seedling out lovely. (*Fore runner*).
Mar 21	Went Morwellham via Calstock, Harewood, Gunnislake Bridge and down the Duchy Drive and back about 15 miles and no stop for refreshment.
Mar 26	Doll Jope goes to hospital.
Apr 6	Saw 1st Air ship at night with red light from our door.
Apr 18	Repeat walk!
Apr 23	Went Berry to hear Petterson and Macavoy on wireless.
Apr 30	Received 37 bar ladder and paid 55/- for it.
May 10	2 Bens walked up from Trematon (*brother and young son*)
Dec 4	A Jope down to tell me about our King and a divorce woman.
Dec 13	1st Sunday in the new Rein (*King's reign*).

1937

Jan 6	Went Callington and made a Will.
Feb 1	Miss Betty Jope married Luke Hocking and W Jope and Miss Cox.
Feb 7	Did not go to church and I had a little 'syhatake' (*Sciatica*).
Feb 9	L Hughes and Ida Stephens married.
Mar 18	Butcher Tom Martin died.
Apr 3	Mrs Kitt Berrywood a daughter.
Apr 12	Rev Stretfield came down to see my seedlings.
May 6	W Roberts decarbonised auto culto.
May 12	Coronation went to church in streams of rain it cleared off for the sports, which was jolly good.
May 15	Double whites 1/3.
May 18	W Roberts and Miss Sargeant married. Finished hacking potatoes.
May 30	A Jope and I went Comfort Wood and back through Cleave Gardens and Nattles strawberries were the ripest. Wesleyan anniversary.
June 3	Duke of Windsor married.
June 14	167 2lb. Chips strawberries for market 1/3d chip.
June 19	Miss Vera Rogers and Tamblyn married.
Aug 26	Charlie Ford died and H Langsford's sale (Murdon).

Aug 31	Beans 2/- 1000, apples 1/3 chip (2lb), potatoes 5/- cwt. William (Fiddler) Reep died.
Sept 6	Mrs Williams put 'brassick' on bad leg. (*Borasic*).
Sept 8	Dr Joslin came to Mrs Williams at 3am.
Sept 12	Phyllis Jope wore her false teeth 1st time.
Sept 23	Beans made 4/- 1000 apples ½d and 1d lb. Harvest thanksgiving and paid Deacon (Paynters cross) 11/6 for 4 tool repairs.
Oct 14	Filled out Littlewoods coupon 1st time.
Oct 16	17 points Littlewoods.
Oct 23	18 points.
Oct 30	15 points.
Nov 6	18 points.
Nov 7	Trees looking very pretty leaves very many colours.
Dec 2	Lily Babb and N Rickard married
Dec 4	Sold cow and calf to Jim Reep £16.
Dec 14	Mr Peter Hambly come down for me to come and slip dogs at Viverdon as usual. I lent him the slips and told him not to expect me. (But I may).
Dec 16	Went to Plymouth and missed coursing 1st time for over 40 years.

St Dominick Mothers' Union

Inez Martin, Jane Veale, Win Olver, Mary Martin, Reverend and Mrs Perry-Gore, Mrs Dawe, Sylvia Mason, Kathleen Martin, Vera Studden, Mabel Herring, Francis Reep, Audrey Babb, Kathleen Borlase. c.1950s.   Courtesy of John Rapson (Liskeard).

CHAPTER TWENTY-THREE

Inez Martin, born in 1919 has written her memories of a childhood spent in Bohetherick, which makes both interesting and amusing reading. Inez kindly agreed for me to print some of her tales. Here in her own words, is her vivid description of family outings and recollections of her grandfather William Martin.

Past Times

by Inez Martin

Inez Martin's late husband Bernard at their home Green Acre.

Outings were few and far between. To go shopping in Plymouth or Devonport, was a great treat, especially when we went by river on the market boat, which was the most convenient way for us as the nearest bus stop was nearly two miles away. It was fun calling at the quays picking up passengers with their goods for sale at the market.

Farmer's wives would be there with baskets filled with butter, cream and eggs and other delicacies, surrounded by crates of cabbages and baskets of fruit. We sat on hard wooden seats, but with so much of interest to see on the way, comfort was not important. When we reached our destination it was like being in another world. To me the large stores were rather frightening. Whilst my mother chose something, I was lifted on to a high chair by the counter. It was one way of keeping me out of mischief. Any desire to shuffle was stifled by the fear of falling off; the floor looked a long way down.

Clothes were cheap compared with current prices. A pair of shoes could be bought for 10/- and a coat for under two pounds. Hats were a very important part of a ladies' wardrobe. It was fashionable to have them lavishly trimmed with flowers, ribbons, feathers or artificial fruit. Plain hats were often chosen and then taken to a milliner for trimming. This way, there was less chance of duplication. Ladies did not like to be seen wearing a hat identical to another one. One hat stands out in my mind more than any other. It came as a complete surprise, when we were on our way home one day. The Captain of the boat, who we knew very well, produced a paper bag containing a girls new hat of cream straw, decorated with tiny white daisies all over the brim. Someone had left it on the boat some weeks before. As it had not been claimed, he gave it to me. I was so thrilled I could hardly wait until the next Sunday, to wear it. There must have been a very disappointed little girl somewhere, but I was too young to give it any thought.

The Sunday school I attended provided a treat for us each summer, usually to the seaside. Great preparations were made the day before, with kitchens filled with appetising smells of pasties and cakes, in readiness for packing up next morning. Apple pasties were very popular, accompanied by fresh cream.

On the morning of departure, we all met at the appointed place to await the arrival of the charabancs, which were far different from the coaches on the road today. The tyres were solid and could be heard rumbling from a long way off. Long leather seats stretched across the charabanc, with their own doors on one side. When everyone was seated, we set off on our journey, hoping for a fine day. The only protection from the rain, was the canvas hood folded concertina fashion at the back. It was quite a performance pulling it over the top, so very often before it was fixed, we were wet anyway! A mile or two from home, our excitement rose as we watched for a familiar figure, perched on the hedge with a camera. This was Mr Gimblett from Callington, waiting to take our photographs. There was some delay here, as there were always four or five 'charas' and the manipulation of the camera, set up on a tripod, was a slow procedure. At last, when the old man was satisfied, he draped the black cloth over his head and clicked away.

'Bowser Babb' at Cotehele. c.1920s.

We left him smiling happily, probably contemplating the number of orders he would get for his pictures. He must have done very well, because he appeared every year. Some of the photographs are still around. Fashion-wise, they are amusing to look at. Ladies wore their flower bedecked hats and the men their best clothes and caps. Our destination was never more than twenty or thirty miles away, but it seemed a long journey to us, we only travelled about twenty miles an hour.

When we eventually arrived at the seaside, it was a great race to the beach; after all, we only saw the sea once or twice a year. We were allowed to take our shoes and socks off to paddle in the sea, but nothing so adventurous as bathing. We had to be content with watching other people. I can just remember the old bathing machines, used for changing in. They were drawn along by ponies, to the edge of the water, so that the bathers could step straight into the sea. It was considered indelicate to walk across the crowded beach in a bathing costume! Compared with bikinis and the minute trunks worn today, the bathers were almost fully clothed. Costumes were made of thick black or navy blue material, reaching below the knee, with sleeves to the elbows. Some of the men wore bold striped creations, making them look like so many zebras bobbing about in the sea! There was so much to see and do on the beach that we were always reluctant to leave. After we had raided the food baskets, we set off on a visit to the shops, with the main purpose of buying presents to take home. Pieces of china decorated with a coat of arms, were firm favourites. We bought them for a few pence and now they have become collectors items and quite expensive to buy. One lady, who usually went on our outings, spent most of the day buying gifts for her family. She could afford much better things than most of us. She bought ornate vases, decorated cups and saucers and other novelties in china and glass. I remember her showing me a milk jug in the shape of a cow, with it's tail forming the handle. I thought how wonderful it would be to take home something like that. However, I was happy with my cheap present, which I guarded carefully on the way home.

Cotehele Quay is still one of my favourite spots. I used to spend a lot of time there with my grandfather, William Martin, who had worked on barges on the river all his life. His barge the 'Myrtle' berthed at Cotehele between her journeys to Millbay Docks at Plymouth. For many years after trading had ceased, the old quay looked shabby and forgotten now, thanks to the National Trust, it has come to life again. The old building used as a store by Grandfather, is now a Museum,

Cap'n Bill Martin and his barge 'Myrtle' at Cotehele Quay. His son Harry Martin is fixing the mast. The boy on the bicycle is Gerald Langsford. 'Myrtle' was the last barge to ply the River Tamar. *c.* early 1920s.

exhibiting relics and pictures of barges which were once a common sight on the river. Close by, one of the veterans of the Tamar, The Shamrock, now restored to her former glory, floats again as another reminder of days gone by. This well maintained beauty spot now attracts thousands of visitors each year. The old stone built cottages and lime kilns, contrast sharply, with the cars and general characters of modern life. But when the visitors have gone, the quay seems to slip back in time, showing scarcely a trace of change. The attractive Lodge overlooking the quay lies at the foot of the drive leading to Cotehele House. This lovely old mansion was once the home of the Edgcumbe family for over five hundred years.

When I was a child it was always a thrill to catch a glimpse of the Earl and Countess, as they were driven in their horse-drawn carriage on their way to take up residence at Cotehele.

My mother was Win Olver and she used to visit Cotehele Quay when her father's barge was in dock. One day when she was a little girl, an incident occurred which could have cost her life. It happened on the occasion that King Edward VII and Queen Alexandra visited the Earl and Countess of Mount Edgcumbe at Cotehele House. They came by yacht to Cotehele Quay and my grandfather's barge was moved out of the dock to allow the yacht in. My mother was among the spectators on the 'Myrtle' eagerly waiting to see the Royal visitors. As they approached, an error of judgement by the pilot resulted in a collision with the barge. Someone pulled my mother back just in time, from where the damage was caused. I do not know any details, but grandfather was compensated for the incident.

My grandfather's love of his work was reflected in the way he looked after the 'Myrtle'. After each consignment, the hold was cleaned out ready for the next journey to Plymouth. Painting and general repairs were promptly attended to. When barges depended on the elements for propulsion it was important to inspect the sails and ropes regularly. Grandfather was an expert at splicing ropes, a craft his father taught him.

The men who lived on the quay always kept an eye on the barge, if there was no one else around. I clearly remember being roused in the early hours, by a voice calling, "Cap'n Bill, you'd better come down, the 'Myrtle' is up on the quay." Rough weather and high tides occasionally caused the barge to be partially lifted off the dock, on to the quay.

The bearer of the news was always a man known locally as 'Bowser' Babb. He had to walk over half a mile to our house, which shows the concern people had for each other.

Grandfather sold the 'Myrtle' to Harold Langsford in 1925, but the Martin family continued to man the barge on his behalf. My grandfather Cap'n Bill Martin died in 1932 and I have very fond memories of him and my grandmother.

1938

Jan 25	Saw Northern lights.
Feb 17	Heard the King on the wireless.
Feb 22	Arthur Rabbage and Miss R Langsford married.
May 17	Queen Mary at Cotehele.
May 26	Phyllis and I went Bath and West Show.
June 26	Fred Rabbage died.
Sept 1	Went to Lands End.

Valentine (Tiny) Traise. A cobbler at Radland Ford. c.1930s.

CHAPTER TWENTY-FOUR

In the following chapter Peter Langsford tells the story of what happened to the barge 'Myrtle' after it was purchased from Cap'n Bill Martin by Harold Langsford.

Barges

by Peter Langsford

The sailing barge 'Myrtle' was built at Bob May's yard at Ashburton Quay, Calstock in 1896 for Cap'n Bill Martin (1860–1932) of Bohetherick. Cap'n Bill was the chief barge owner and operator on the River Tamar at that time. He also owned two other barges, 'Martin' and 'Secret'. Cap'n Bill's father was in the barge business before him.

In 1900 a barge was built by Hawkes Shipyard at Plymouth at the request of Charles Langsford junior. It cost £300 and was named 'Dorothy' after one of Charles Langsford's daughters, (Mrs Harold Maunder). However this barge did not feature in the valuation when Charles's son Harold, my father, took over from his father in 1914. Apparently, it had been sold and moved to another location at Falmouth. For a number of years the Langsford family used the Martin's barges to haul their grain to Glamorgan and Cotehele Mills. In 1925 Harold Langsford purchased the barge 'Myrtle' from Cap'n Bill Martin, but he and his son, Harry continued to man the barge till about 1930 when Cap'n Bill retired. At that time, Harry's son Ronald joined his father's crew. Ronald had previously worked at Cotehele Mill.

Sailing up the River Tamar by wind and tide was a time consuming business. The barge often managed to get within sight of Cotehele Quay and had to moor off owing to a turn of the tide or lack of favourable wind. The barge could only dock at Cotehele Quay at high tide.

By 1926 the sails had fallen into disrepair, so Harold Langsford had a marine 'Kelvin' engine installed and also the hand winch was replaced by a motor winch by Hamworthy of Poole, the work being carried out by Chas. Cload of Plymouth. During the period 1914–1939 when Cotehele Mill was in its heyday, the barge was very busy hauling goods up the Tamar from Plymouth Docks. Maize from the River Plate in South America and Bessarabia (Romania in North-East Russia), barley from Persia; This was so dry and hard that it could not be ground by millstones unless it was softened

Harold Langsford, Jack Coles, Harry Martin, in the rose garden at Morden (Cotehele) Mill. c.1940s.

and swollen by water at a rate of about five per cent. This was an added bonus for the miller, so today's addition of water to packets of ham and bacon, is nothing new! Leonard Hughes, the local blacksmith remarked that, 'every time the waterwheel went round, it put another six-pence in Harold Langsford's pocket!'

Then there was French wheat, the price of which went down to £4 a ton at one time. Coal also came up river in the barge; fifty-ton loads were delivered to George Langsford's store at Cotehele and to Plymouth Co-op at Halton Quay. The haulage charge was 2/6d (12½p in today's money) per ton, £6.50 for a fifty ton load. Out of this came the wage for two bargemen, plus one extra man winching up the baskets and another two in the hold, shovelling the coal into the baskets.

Occasionally there was a load of lightweight foreign timber logs for Cotehele sawmill. This was sawn out by Mr Bill Roberts, the sawyer, and used for making boxes for local market gardeners. Bill Roberts also built the bodywork on Model T Ford chassis. Harold Langsford had two of these trucks, each capable of carrying 10 sacks of maize, one ton, as each sack contained two cwt. George Langsford used one in his coal business and Horatio Langsford of Murdon Farm and Joe Snell at Radland also had this type of truck. All the five bar gates for the Cotehele Estate were made at the mill by Bill Roberts, using local oak or chestnut. When more timber was needed Harold Langsford and Bill would go down to the wood with Lord Mount Edgcumbe's estate agent, Captain F McClure-Williams, to select a suitable tree. After it was felled, it was cut into logs and dragged from the wood to the lower saw bench at Cotehele Mill. There was a two wheel contraption, called a 'devil', which lifted the front of a log off the ground on a chain, making it easier for the horse to drag it from the wood to the sawmill. The logs were sawn on the rack bench, into planks about three inches thick and left to season for a year or two. When seasoned they were taken to the top bench and sawn into suitable lengths for making gates. Adjoining the upper saw-bench was a workshop, containing a mortising machine and a machine for sharpening circular saws, all driven by water power. The second waterwheel which was installed by Charles Langsford, at his own expense in the late 19th century, was not used after the Second World War and was demolished. When Harold Langsford took over from his father in 1914 he paid £300 to his father's estate, which was the cost of building the workshops and punnet shop and water wheel. There were no forge or wheelwrights at the mill in those days; they were added when the property was surrendered to the National Trust by me in 1960. The Langsfords had been the tenants of Cotehele Mill for almost 100 years, and the irony was, that I paid dilapidations on the buildings, most of which had been built by my family.

The 'Myrtle' met a sad ending. The barge was commandeered during the Second World War and was used for carrying goods in Devonport Dockyard. It was destroyed by incendiary bombs during the Plymouth blitz and that was the end of the last barge that carried goods up the River Tamar.

Eight year old Peter Langsford with his latest invention, an outdoor stove! c.1926.

CHAPTER TWENTY-FIVE

Whilst helping me uncover the Langsford family history and the story of the corn mills, Peter Langsford often spoke of incidents which occurred during his time in the army during the Second World War. The years he spent abroad differed so much from the quiet lifestyle of the villagers he left behind, that I felt his war-time experiences might well be of interest to readers. The following chapter includes some of Peter's recollections leading up to the time when he took over the milling business from his father.

Wars and Waterwheels

by Peter Langsford

Peter Langsford the last mill owner of St Dominick. c.1947.

I was born in 1918, the only son of Harold and Dorothy Langsford, *née* Cradick. I spent my early years in the miller's house at Cotehele, with my three sisters. My father was a miller as were my grandfather and great-grandfather. I left Callington School when I was seventeen and was very interested in chemistry, but I was not encouraged to study the subject further and was expected to carry on the family tradition and work in the milling business in some capacity.

I took over the office work, but developed pleurisy in my late teens and suffered with chest problems for some time. A combination of dust from the mill and the chill dampness of the position of our home did nothing to improve my health. We moved to nearby Bartletts to live in 1938 and a year later I passed my medical and joined the Army.

My eldest sister Marie, married Douglas Martin in 1942 and they had three daughters, Virginia, Sally and Mary. Nancy married Ernest Reep and their two daughters are Josephine and Katryn. My youngest sister Joyce, married Ralph Varco and they are both dead now, but left two sons, Peter and John.

In September 1939 I was called for compulsory Military Service. 'MILITIA' was intended for six months duration, but as war was declared on 3rd September I was *in*, so had to make the best of it. I was sent to Exeter, to the Devonshire Regiment where I did basic square bashing etc. until Christmas. For two months I drove the billeting officer around Exeter paying out money to local householders who were compelled to take in soldiers, as there was not enough room in the barracks. I was billeted with Mr and Mrs Knowles. Three of us in the room sleeping on the floor, one of whom was a useless drunkard and rogue who was very often sick all over the room. There were a lot of rough ones in that lot, I had never heard the 'F' word before, but some of them did not know many other words than that. Remember, I was sent to Miss Beatrice Quint's Dame School at Calstock up to the age of about eight where in addition to the 3Rs, we were taught dancing, piano playing, painting and other genteel subjects! It was quite a shock to me to be landed in the Army. My pay at that time was 10/- a week of which we were given 8/-, the balance being held back for toothpaste, boot polish, Blanco etc. On one occasion the Billeting Officer, who was a very pleasant chap offered me a tip of 2/6d after driving him around Exeter, but I refused to take it. I was always very independent, beholding to no one and managed very well on my pay. I did not smoke or drink but did go out for a few meals, barrack room food was awful. I went to Dellers Restaurant in Exeter High Street on my 21st birthday and had roast pheasant, I think it cost 4/-.

From 15th January 1940 to 17th October 1940, I was Assistant Company Accountant. We were at Golden Hill Fort, Freshwater, Isle of Wight during this period. All we had to do was keep the pay records of the company. To do that there was a Company Quartermaster Sergeant, Sergeant Rooke, three ATS girls and myself! I could have done it on my own in an hour and the five of us had a week to do it. There were Parades to attend of course. It was very cold that winter and we spent a lot of time piling coke into the tortoise stoves in the barrack rooms; no shortage of coke, which was a blessing. Also we had a spell on the hill behind Ventnor guarding an early warning radar station, very cold indeed stuck outside for two hours at a time in a blizzard.

We returned to Denbury Camp at Newton Abbot in the spring of 1940. I was still in the office doing very little. Newton Abbot Station was bombed at this time. We saw the 'Dorniers' go over our camp and took to the slit trenches, the RSM was first in! They did not drop anything on us, but we heard the bombs go off at the station. Several nice houses were damaged and some people killed. Newton Abbot was a quite important railway junction.

From Denbury I was sent to an officer cadet training unit in Llandrindod Wells in Wales. Very hard going for sixteen weeks, but I survived and came out as 2nd Lieutenant in the Royal Artillery. Eventually, after a spell at Woolwich Barracks I boarded a ship at Liverpool and after a long sea trip landed at Suez. During the sea journey we landed at Cape Town and were given a wonderful reception and also went into Durban where a famous lady came out on the Quayside and sang patriotic songs through a megaphone. She wore flowing white clothes and they called her Aunty Durban. She did this for every troopship that came into Durban.

A very hot train ride across the desert from Suez took me to Cairo to a place called El-tahag, which was a camp in the desert on the outskirts of Cairo city. You could catch a tram within walking distance and get into the city centre. The tram stop was near an ice cream parlour called Groppies where we got the most wonderful ice cream sundaes. My favourite was a Josephine Baker which cost me 2/-, but I could easily afford that as I was on Lieutenants pay of $4 a week. The cinema was the only cool spot in Cairo being air-conditioned. I saw 'Fantasia' and 'Snow White and the Seven Dwarfs' in there.

After Cairo we were sent to Cyprus where we joined a unit, 20 AA Battery, which had escaped from Greece when the Germans took over. There was no accommodation for us at Famagusta and for a while we slept in trenches on our ground-sheets. Later we got some tents and Nissan huts and we set up camp in a pine forest about two miles NE of Famagusta town. Our camp was on ground belonging to Mr Theo Mogabgab and his sister Miss Matilda Mogabgab. He was in charge of Antiquities and excavations in that area. They became very good friends of mine and I often went over to their bungalow for tea. She made me a lovely banana cake once. Their ancestors were High Priests of Moab.

Also near the camp were orange gardens belonging to the Kounnas family. I became good friends with them all. They had a son called Vasili (Basil). He was quite enterprising and opened a café in his orange garden and also allowed us to go over for hot showers or baths, It was not possible to export any oranges at that time, so they just rotted on the ground. We all had as many as we wanted, free. After the war I went back to Cyprus and was entertained most royally by Basil Kounnas who had become quite rich as they were the Kounnas Bros., quite big in the orange export business. He even lent me one of his cars to tour the island. One friend of mine got drunk at the Limassol Wine Festival. We carried him back to the hotel where he was unconscious for two days. During the war Cyprus red wine 'Commandaria' was 2/- a bottle. Just imagine the drunkenness.

We did not man the guns at night and apart from the guard we could all go to town. Our four 4.7 inch static Ack-Ack guns arrived in Cyprus shortly after we arrived there. We had to dig the gunpits and bring the guns up from the docks and get them installed. We never fired those guns, as any enemy aircraft that came over were too high and out of range at 32,000 feet. Our range was

30,000 feet! Some Italians bombed Famagusta harbour and some of our men were killed down there, I was fortunate not to have been down at the harbour that day.

When Rommel was in the Western Desert threatening Egypt and the Suez Canal and Middle East oil supplies, we were brought back to Egypt to defend the Suez Canal. My Battery the 20th, was at Port Said, two miles west of the canal near the beach, so one could keep cool there. If any enemy planes came over they were still out of range and we were ordered not to fire any guns for fear of exposing our position to enemy reconnaissance planes and to save ammunition. One day though, when I was in charge of the Command post, the Italians came over very high and out of range as usual. We were all so bored with polishing guns, white washing stones that bordered the Camp road and attending the flytraps, that I gave the order 'FIRE'. This happened just as the Battery Commander, Major Newey, (Zip Fasteners, Birmingham) came up the coast road in his staff-car and saw the guns firing. I got a mild raspberry for disobeying orders. I was quite popular with the gun crews after that, as everyone was bored with just sitting there, not banging off!

Our gun emplacements were just built up with sandbags, so the powers above ordered that the sandbags were to be faced inside with masonry and Egyptian stonemasons were employed to do the work. They really were wonderful craftsmen. The stones they used were cut into rough hexagons and all beautifully fitted together. Their wages were ten piastres, commonly called 'ackers' or 2/- a day and so poor that they scavenged food from our swill bins and their clothes were just old rags and sacking. Englishmen were not supposed to have any sympathy for the natives at that time and because I did and gave them my fag ration (which I did not want), I was nicknamed 'Woggi', a name which stuck until I left the Army.

One day the Brigade Major came up from Moascar to Port Said and asked me if I would like a spell at Brigade H.Q. as Intelligence Officer and as I was fed up with Port Said and ready for a change, I readily accepted.

We lived in a very nice, newly built house down there with all facilities and servants. Also we were able to swim in the Suez Canal everyday and go sailing on Lake Timsah. There wasn't much to do except ride up and down the one hundred mile long road beside the Suez Canal and put coloured pins in the Brigadier's map, so that he knew where everyone was. He was Brigadier W Gordon Black, the boss of Blacks Tents and Linoleum, (Nairns).

After that I was in a similar job in Cairo, for Brigadier Wilson at Air H.Q. I had accommodation in a sort of hotel, Anglo-Swiss Pension. It was there that I became very ill and was put in hospital, first in the 63rd General Hospital, Cairo, and later in Jerusalem in Kaiser Bill's Palace on the Mount of Olives. (He was Emperor of Germany before the First World War). Those of us who did not die were later evacuated to South Africa, travelling from Jerusalem to Suez by train and from there to Durban by ship, thence by train to Johannesburg Baragwanath Military Hospital about 15 miles from the city. It was a wonderful climate down there, but I had no treatment for my tuberculosis except fresh air and plenty of rest. I did a lot of knitting, baby suits, which I sent home for my nieces Josephine and Virginia. I also made a lot of Fairisle pullovers and I knitted a ladies dress on size 16 needles with two ply wool in feather and fan stitch, for my cousin Winifred Klatzow, the daughter of my father's eldest sister. I got first prize at the National Eistedfodd of Johannesburg in 1944 for my knitting! I also collected stamps and took up piano playing as we had a piano in the occupational therapy department.

Some of us had periods of convalescence in houses in the smart northern suburbs of the city. Many of the rich people out there, especially the Jews, were very patriotic and gladly allowed us to have their houses.

Many of the nurses in that hospital were the daughters of rich South Africans who volunteered their services. One nurse in particular, with whom I was quite friendly invited me to go to the Cape Province and stay with her parents at their Estate about fifty miles from Capetown. They had large fruit growing estates both in Cape Province and in Natal. Their house was large and in the Dutch Colonial style and all their servants wore livery. There were no sons in that household and I think they were looking for an Englishman for their daughter to marry! This girl did marry an English sailor. I met them once at Mount Edgcumbe, where they had a cottage, but I do not know what happened to them after that. The girl's father had been in the First World War and married her mother who was heiress to estates and business interests in Capetown. They were very patriotic and very English and did not speak with a South African accent.

While I was in the Army I think I forgot the St Dominick lingo completely. In fact, my own father could not understand me when I came home! I think I have re-learnt it now.

Just think, I might have become the boss of vast South African acres, hordes of Hottentot workers and everything that goes with it! However, the homing instinct got the better of me, so I eventually returned home in 1947. What struck me most as we sailed up Southampton Water, was the extreme greenness of everything and on that train back to Tavistock I heard the West Country accent which seemed very strange indeed. I had been away about seven years altogether, which when you are young seemed a very long time – Nowadays the years just fly by.

I had a relapse of my TB when I returned home and spent another two years at home or at Brompton Hospital in London and the King Edward VII Sanatorium at Midhurst.

I eventually came home to the mill business in 1949, first in partnership with Father and when he retired, on my own. I must admit I loathed the business, but made the best of it. I took on two representatives to call on customers and built two new stores at Glamorgan Mill. By now, Cotehele Mill was out of date and quite useless as a mill. I brought three-phase electric supply to Glamorgan Mill so that all the grinding was powered by electricity and the millstones and waterwheel were thrown out. Thanks to the loyalty of staff, especially Charlie Sambles and after his death, his widow Georgie and Gilbert Burley and their hard work and efficiency, we managed to increase the business, particularly in sales of Spillers animal foods. It was a pity that the waterwheel which was in excellent working order, was demolished, but at the time it seemed the only thing to do to make room for more modern gear.

The demise of country mill businesses was already on the cards and in 1969, I sold out to Spillers. The lorries and stock at valuation, new buildings at cost and the old mill for a nominal sum, plus a small amount for goodwill. Spillers did not run the mill very long, they combined it with another business at Lee Mill in Devon. I retained the book debts of about £50,000 and managed to collect in all of it except about £50. £50,000 was quite a large sum then, as the average price of goods sold was about £30 a ton, now it is ten times that amount. Spillers sold the old mill and the new stores, I think they got about £16,000 for it and the purchaser made it into a dwelling house. Later the mill and outbuildings were sold on to the present owner and a lot of money has been spent there. One store is used as a factory called Mill Windows and the other store is owned by James Evans, the railway preservation expert and of apple tree fame. I also sold the house called Bartletts when my mother died in 1976. I was not sorry to get out of the valley and I now live in a small bungalow in St Dominick village, but I drive down that beautiful valley several times a week for nostalgic reasons and look back to those days at Cotehele Mill before the war, when we were a very happy family there. It was a busy place and we had a very good life-style.

It is now 1999 and approaching the Millennium. I have been retired since I was fifty years old and have had thirty years in retirement with nothing to do but play the Stock Exchange. I am quite sure that I have done better at that than I ever could have done at the mill.

The only thing I now own which once belonged to my great-grandfather, is 22 acres of land, which was part of Cleave Farm where he lived and died. My father bought it from a subsequent owner of Cleave Farm for £100 an acre and I bought it from him for £200 an acre. At present it is let to two farmers, so I suppose I can call myself a Landlord.

In the late 19th and early 20th centuries there were literally dozens of Langsfords living down the Valley and now there are none. Zena and William, my cousins, who lived at Newhouses, have both died recently, in the house where their grandmother had lived. Before that they had lived at Morden Farm. I, Peter Langsford am the last in the Parish to bear the Langsford name and the only direct descendant of Charles Langsford 1817–1902, still living in Cotehele Valley is my niece, the well-known artist Mary Martin.

CHAPTER TWENTY-SIX

Full Circle

by Natalie Allen

I write this final chapter during the last hours of the millennium, filled with a mixture of sadness and hope.

So much has happened in the village over the past one hundred and fifty years. More changes have taken place in the 20th century than had occurred over the previous five hundred years.

When in the late 1860s a St Dominick man, Walter Lawry visited London and became aware of the viability of selling his strawberries to markets in that city, little did he realise just how big an impact his pioneering idea would have on growers in the Tamar Valley. With the arrival of the railways which provided a cheap and efficient means of transport, soon a large percentage of the crops produced on the fertile slopes of the Tamar, were being despatched to markets all over England. The higher prices received, well outweighed the expense of transportation and the sales were a welcome addition to the grower's income, which had previously been restricted by local demand at Plymouth and Devonport. The market gardeners flourished. With hard-work and dedication generations of local families made a living off the land.

Subsidiary industries grew up alongside the gardens. In the early days the need for fertilizer meant that the sweepings from the streets of Plymouth, known locally as 'dock dung' was brought on barges to the quays at Cotehele and Halton, and transported by horse and cart to the market gardens. Lime kilns provided work, as did the cottage industry of punnet making. Sawmills produced timber for box making and tools were made and repaired by local blacksmiths. Carpenters were needed to make the huge ladders required to harvest cherries and apples from the trees, which were grown in abundance. Casual labour provided work for young and old at peak times and most families became almost self-sufficient.

But times have changed. 'Progress' has meant the loss of a means of transport as the 'Beeching' axe closed local railway freight stations. Britain's entry into the Common Market brought an influx of cheap flowers; fruit and vegetables into the Country, with little hope of export prospects for local growers, to compensate. High wages in other jobs led to young people deserting the land to work in less arduous circumstances. Television and the possibility to travel abroad made the narrow lives of their parents and grandparents seem dull and unexciting and the younger generation began to seek entertainment and partners well away from the village confines.

The inter-marriage of local families in the past, meant that familiar names predominated, but now as new houses continue to be built at the Churchtown end of the village and newcomers move in, new names well outstrip the old.

My own family name of Langsford is now confined to one bachelor in St Dominick and other once familiar names have already died out completely.

The lime kilns, corn mills, horticultural store, garages, undertaker, butcher shops, carpenters, wheelwright and Trinity Chapel are gone. The market gardens at Brentswood, Comfort Wood and the Cotehele valley which were ripped with such effort and hopefulness by our ancestors, have turned full circle and returned once more to woodland. The choir, who once sang in Brentswood on that warm July day, is now silent. The only reminder of the hard-working men and women who spent their lives toiling on the steep slopes, is a rusty packing shed, the image of which I captured on my last visit to Brentswood in 1996.

But all is not lost. The Church, Ebenezer Chapel, the Pub and the Post Office still remain as focal points in the village. As this book goes to print Brian Rickard who recently took over Lanoyce Nurseries from his parents Alan and Joyce Rickard, has been short listed for a top National Award by 'Grower' magazine in respect of his modern approach to growing alstroemeria under glass.

In 1989, Lanoyce was also the first nursery in the United Kingdom to introduce artificial light to induce high quality winter crops. Now more than 60% of its 15,000 square metres of glass is lit. Although the small market gardens have practically died out in St Dominick, its two large nurseries Sunningdale and Lanoyce continue to be worked by family members of three well-known growers of the past, Westlake Rickard, Harold Harris and Frances Hunn. Methods have changed enormously but flowers do still bloom in the valley, albeit now sheltered from unpredictable weather conditions thus making for easier harvesting.

Two 'newcomers' namely Ann Murphy of Radland House and Alistair Tinto of Lower Berry Cottage have already fallen under the spell of our old village. Their interest in local history will ensure its past will not be forgotten.

Hopefully, some young person in the village will decide to keep a daily record of the everyday happenings as Joe Snell did seventy years ago.

Meanwhile the newly planted conifers and self-sown scrubland hide the secrets of a century of hard working men and women. As Joe and our much loved ancestors rest in the nearby churchyard, so rests the soil, awaiting a new awakening and a new millennium …

Joe Snell's grave in St Dominick churchyard. c.1999.